Top 20 Parents

Raising Happy, Responsible & Emotionally Healthy Children

Paul Bernabei   Sharon Kaniess   Elaine Rilley
Tom Cody   Mary Cole   Michael Cole   Willow Sweeney

Designed and Illustrated by Tim Parlin

Top 20 Press St. Paul, MN

an imprint of Morgan James Publishing, LLC • New York

ISBN: 978-0-97428-431-6
1. Parenting. 2. Children. 3. Emotionally healthy.
Publisher's Cataloging-in-Publication Data
Bernabei, Paul.
Top 20 parents: raising happy, responsible and emotionally healthy children /Paul Bernabei …
(et al.); designed and illustrated by: Tim Parlin. St. Paul, MN:Top 20 Press, 2008

Published by:
Top 20 Training, St. Paul, Minnesota
an imprint of

MORGAN · JAMES
THE ENTREPRENEURIAL PUBLISHER ™
www.morganjamespublishing.com

Morgan James Publishing, LLC
1225 Franklin Ave. Ste 325
Garden City, NY 11530-1693
Toll Free 800-485-4943
www.MorganJamesPublishing.com

To learn more about Top 20 Training or to order additional copies of Top 20Parents or Top 20 Teens, email us at: info@top20training or call (651) 690-5758.

As an Early Childhood Special Education Teacher and a mother of two young boys, *Top 20 Parents* has taught me to re-frame the way I look at different situations with myself, my children, my husband and my students. It has enabled me to be a better parent, wife and teacher.

–Gina Paton ECSE Teacher, St. Paul Public Schools

Top 20 Parents has given us practical tools to handle the complex challenges of parenting a growing child. We continually go back to the basic principles that have empowered us to create a strong, nurturing family. This book provides an intentional, initial 'blue print' for a healthy family life and is an excellent problem solving reference.

–Ellen and Richard Hendrick, PhD., parents

"*Top 20 Parents* has taught me to approach problems related to my children in a healthy way. When my child misbehaves, whines or does something unacceptable at preschool, I now look at the situation in a calm and non-judgmental way."

–Kaoru Kinoshita Adachi, mother,
Ph. D. Student, Comparative and International Development Education

Origins and Acknowledgements

Many core concepts presented in *Top 20 Parents* are adapted from the work of Top 20 Training. Founded by Paul Bernabei, Tom Cody, Mary Cole, Michael Cole and Willow Sweeney in 2000, Top 20 Training conducts workshops throughout the United States to empower youth and adults to develop their potential. These trainings present easily understood principles that are readily applicable to everyday parenting and family situations.

Sharon Kaniess and Elaine Rilley attended a Top 20 training session in 2003. Since then they have augmented the Top 20 concepts with information and insights from many years as teachers in Minnesota's unique Early Childhood Family Education Program (ECFE).

As authors, we wish to acknowledge the generosity of youth and adults who shared their wisdom and stories with the Top 20 team. We further acknowledge our mentors and peers in St. Paul and throughout Minnesota who have passed on their experiences to us. Because some of the parenting information presented in this book has developed over many years and from numerous sources, we are not always sure where some ECFE sayings originated.

We are also grateful to the families who have attended our ECFE classes. Their stories and quotes are included in *Top 20 Parents* with the names changed. In writing this book, we have dipped into the wealth of other parenting books in order to bring the best overview possible of Top 20 parenting tools.

We are especially grateful to our own parents, spouses, children and grandchildren who have taught us the profound importance of family.

Preface

Our purpose in writing *Top 20 Parents* is to enhance the quality of the parenting journey and develop the incredible potential in each child and family. This book provides parents with awareness and tools to create more enjoyable and productive experiences with their young children.

Each chapter, except Chapters 1 and 18, contains four parts:

Story: A family scenario is presented at the beginning of each chapter. This short story reveals the context relating to the main concept presented in the chapter.

Concept: The majority of each chapter explains concepts or tools to empower parents to make a positive difference in their lives and the lives of their children. Many of these concepts can also be used in adult relationships or work experiences.

Developmental News Flash: Parents want to know more about their children's development. The Developmental News Flash section helps parents to have realistic expectations of their children by better understanding the interplay between behavior and development. Readers are also encouraged to use the many sources about child development available in libraries and bookstores and on the internet.

Time for Action: Parents also want practical ideas to use in real life situations. The Time for Action section at the end of each chapter includes suggestions and strategies for learning the Top 20 parenting style and raising Top 20 kids.

Gender pronouns are alternated throughout the book.

About the Authors

Sharon H. Kaniess has worked with early childhood, elementary and high school students for 20 years. She has taught in St. Paul's Early Childhood Family Education Program for 15 years. A graduate of Dr. Martin Luther College and Concordia University, she has a Masters of Education and is an Early Childhood and School-Age Trainers Association Credentialed Trainer. She and her husband, Daniel, live in St. Paul, with a daughter and son.

Elaine Rilley has been a parent educator in St. Paul's ECFE Program for 23 years. She also taught junior and senior high students for 22 years. Elaine holds a Parent Educator License. She is a graduate of Mary Grove College and has done graduate work at the University of Minnesota and Hamline University. Elaine and her husband, Jim, live in White Bear Lake, Minnesota. They have two adult children and two grandchildren.

In addition to their Top 20 seminar presentations, Paul Bernabei, Tom Cody, Mary Cole, Michael Cole and Willow Sweeney have co-authored *Top 20 Teens: Discovering the Best-kept Thinking, Learning and Communicating Secrets of Successful Teenagers* and training manuals for classroom teachers.

Paul has been a teacher, counselor, administrator and coach for 35 years. He directs Share-A-Life, a program that supports pregnant women in crisis. A graduate of St. John's University, he and his wife, Paula, live in St. Paul. They have four adult daughters and seven grandchildren.

Tom is a life-long educator, serving as a grade school and high school math teacher since 1974. He has developed innovative curriculum programs at Cretin-Derham Hall High School where he has also coached several athletic teams. A graduate of Colorado State University, Tom and his wife, Judy, live in St. Paul and have three sons.

Mary is co-founder of Salon Development Corporation, an international company specializing in business training. For 25 years she has developed educational materials and products provided by her company. She facilitates training sessions with Michael, her husband and business partner.

Michael, co-founder of Salon Development Corporation, has been a seminar educator for 25 years. He has received numerous awards for his contribution in helping thousands of professionals transform their lives. The Coles, who live in St. Paul, have two children and one grandchild.

Willow, a graduate of the University of St. Thomas, has been a high school coach and world cultures and social justice teacher for seven years. Her work with Top 20 focuses on communication and relationship topics. She, her husband Brian, and son live in St. Cloud, Minnesota.

Table of Contents

CHAPTER 1

Top 20 and Bottom 80 Parenting
Developing Our Potential

"Nothing is as easy as it looks."

Parenting is a journey. What do we want our parenting journey to be like? How will we prepare our children for their own life journey? This book offers usable tools and helpful strategies as we embark on one of the most important and difficult journeys in our lives. More importantly, we will become aware of our **potential, the power within us waiting to be activated so as to make a positive difference in the quality of our lives, relationships and experiences.**

WHAT'S OUR DESTINATION?

Have you ever heard of parents holding their newborns and declaring that they hoped to be the worst possible parents ever? Of course not. People intend to be good parents and want the best for their children. Yet, for some, their goals are not realized and the years of parenting bring frustration and disappointment. The hopes, dreams and good intentions stay just out of reach, floating on a sea of uncertainty.

Parenting is, indeed, like embarking on a journey out to sea. As we set out on calm and serene waters, the journey appears smooth and our dreams reachable. However, we may soon find the sky turning gray and the waves getting rough. When a storm suddenly arrives, we see menacing dark clouds and feel the winds tossing us about. Our anxiety increases as we wonder if we can keep on course. Sometimes more severe storms bear down upon us and we fear we will be lost at sea. It is at these moments in our journey that we may wonder if we should have started the voyage at all.

Parenting is not as easy as it looks. Adele Faber and Elaine Mazlish begin their book, *How to Talk So Kids Will Listen and Listen So Kids Will Talk,* by saying, "I was a wonderful parent before I had children. I was an expert on why everyone else was having problems with theirs. Then I had three of my own. Living with real children can be humbling."[1]

If we start our parenting journey with just good intentions and nothing else, we may quickly find ourselves lost at sea. The purpose of *Top 20 Parents* is to help us manage the challenges that will occur on the parenting journey and arrive at our most desirable destination.

OUR PARENTING TOOL BOX

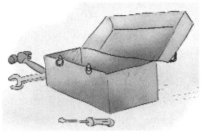

Each of us is the primary builder of our lives. As builders, we all carry a tool box. When we become parents, we are responsible for giving our children tools we have acquired to build their lives.

This book will discuss many tools for building and strengthening our lives as parents and tools to give our children to help them reach their potential. These tools will help us and our children better understand ourselves and build strong relationships with each other. They are the tools for Top 20 Parenting that will develop the tremendous potential in our family.

BECOMING A TOP 20 PARENT

What makes the difference between the Top 20 and Bottom 80? Top 20 people **T**hink, **L**earn and **C**ommunicate (TLC) differently than Bottom 80 people. Our Top 20 TLC results in our functioning at our best and developing our potential. Everyone has the capacity to TLC as a Top 20.

When our thinking, learning and communicating are not serving us well, we are not functioning in our best interest or developing our potential. We are now operating as a Bottom 80. In each situation in our lives, we can operate as a Top 20 and use our TLC to enrich the quality of our lives, relationships and experiences or we can operate as a Bottom 80 and use our TLC to diminish the quality of our lives, relationships and experiences.

Whenever we talk about Top 20 and Bottom 80 in this book, we are not intending to compare people or families. The Top 20/Bottom 80 construct is not about comparing one child to another or one parent to another. Rather, it is a means by which we can grow in awareness of our thinking, learning and communicating and how they are or are not serving our best interest and exploding our potential in wonderful ways.

Each of us is a Top 20 **and** a Bottom 80. When we TLC in highly effective ways, we are operating as a Top 20. When we TLC in highly ineffective ways, we are operating as a Bottom 80. Therefore, when we refer to Top 20 Parenting, we mean that a parent is operating out of his or her Top 20 self and thinking, learning and communicating in highly effective ways. When we refer to Bottom 80 Parenting, we mean that a parent is operating out of his or her Bottom 80 self and thinking, learning and communicating in highly ineffective ways.

The purpose of this book is to become more aware of Top 20 and Bottom 80 ways of thinking, learning and communicating. With that awareness we will more frequently make choices to parent as a Top 20. Obviously, our parenting journey will be a different experience if we are more often operating as a Top 20 than a Bottom 80.

TIME FOR ACTION!

For Parents to Do:

1. Reflect on your journey as a parent. Are you in calm waters with a clear sense of direction? Are you in stormy seas with a hurricane bearing down on you? Are you drifting without direction?

2. Identify how you currently Think, Learn and Communicate (TLC) in:

   A. Top 20 highly effective ways

   B. Bottom 80 highly ineffective ways

To Do with Your Child:

1. Observe the results when you TLC with your child in Top 20 ways.

2. Observe the results when you TLC with your child in Bottom 80 ways.

Above and Below the Line
Being Aware of Our Thinking

*"When Mommy ain't happy,
ain't nobody happy!"*

"Yummy," says Jamie after eating the freshly baked cookie his mom had given him. Hurrying back to the kitchen to ask for more, he smiles at his mom and points to the plate of cooling cookies. "More?"

"Sure, have another one. I'm glad you like my cookies," she says. Happily, Jamie heads off to eat his cookie on the sofa in the next room.

When the phone rings, Jamie hears his mom talking about work. He hears the word "layoff", but has no idea what it means. When she gets off the phone, Jamie runs into the kitchen to ask for another cookie, confident that will make her happy.

"Another cookie? Don't be a pig!" Mom's voice gets louder and scarier. "Were you eating that cookie on the new sofa? I've told you a million times not to eat on the new sofa. Don't you get it? Now clean up your crumbs before I really lose it!"

Feeling his mom's anger, Jamie thinks he's to blame for her mood swing. As he runs out of the kitchen, he kicks the trash can and yells something about the "stupid, yucky cookies."

It is a sobering thought that how we treat our children depends upon how we are feeling ourselves. Much of how our children behave depends upon how they are feeling and how they are treated.

As the story of Jamie and his mom illustrates, being angry about something else in our lives might affect our parenting. Top 20 Parents realize that state of mind, mood and attitude have a powerful influence. They understand the impact these have on their experiences and relationships.

ABOVE AND BELOW THE LINE

The following illustration helps us understand how our state of mind influences our experiences. The horizontal line distinguishes our state of mind as being **Above the Line (ATL) or Below the Line (BTL).**

When we are Above the Line, our state of mind is serving us well and operating in our Best Interest. Because our thinking is working well, we will make better judgments and decisions and communicate more effectively. An Above the Line state of mind brings out the best in us as parents and helps us bring out the best in our children. When we are Below the Line, our state of mind is serving us poorly and not in our Best Interest. Because our thinking is not working well, we will make faulty judgments, poor decisions and communicate ineffectively.

ABOVE THE LINE

A positive view on life and how I see the world.
My thinking is in my Best Interest.
Energetic moods and emotions:
- Positive attitudes • True beliefs • Hopefulness
- Optimism • Power to control my life

BELOW THE LINE

A negative view on life and how I see the world.
My thinking is <u>not</u> in my Best Interest.
Depressing moods and emotions:
- Feelings of sadness and anger
- Negative attitudes • False beliefs • Hopelessness
- Pessimism • Powerless victim of life

LIVING AND VISITING

No one is Above the Line all the time. People fluctuate Above and Below. That's neither good nor bad; it's just being human. However, some people **live** ATL. They spend most of their time there and only **visit** Below. Others, however, **live** BTL and only occassionaly **visit** Above.

By understanding and taking responsibility for our Line, we are able to take more control of our lives and enhance our relationships and experiences.

"I discovered something about myself and my moods. Instead of visiting Above and Below the Line, I had built a permanent house in each place with a connecting driveway. That's expensive. I need to sell the house that's Below the Line."

–A Parent

5

Top 20s and Bottom 80s experience being Below the Line very differently.

When BTL, Top 20s	When BTL, Bottom 80s
• are aware of being Below	• are unaware of being Below
• take responsibility for being BTL	• blame others for being Below
• develop ways to get Above	• stay stuck Below
• don't trust their BTL thinking	• trust their thinking is accurate

MAKING DECISIONS BELOW THE LINE

Another important difference between Top 20 Thinkers and Bottom 80 Thinkers relates to making decisions when Below the Line. **Top 20s don't; Bottom 80s do.** When Jamie's mom went Below, her thinking failed her and she dumped her negativity on her son. Not only were the cookies 'yucky' for Jamie, but she probably felt 'yucky' herself for directing her anger towards her son.

Top 20s avoid making important decisions while they are Below the Line. They wait until they are Above the Line and their thinking is working before they make decisions. Consequently, they make better decisions and don't have to clean up messes or repair damaged relationships. They don't avoid dealing with problems but know they are better problem solvers when they are ATL and their thinking is working in their Best Interest.

Bottom 80s often make decisions when they are BTL and their thinking is not working. The poor decisions create a mess that needs to be cleaned up later. Because she overreacted to Jamie while she was BTL, his mother had to clean up more than cookie crumbs. She spoiled the enjoyable experience she had been having with her son.

"Don't believe everything you think."

CONDITIONS AND EXPERIENCES

Bottom 80s feel like they have little power over the experiences they have each day. They are at the mercy of conditions. They think they can only have a good day if the situations they experience are favorable, like their job status, their children's behavior, the weather or traffic. They claim to be in a bad mood because the conditions aren't right. **The conditions create their experience.**

Top 20s do not view themselves as victims of conditions. Rather, they are aware of their power to determine the experiences they have regardless of the condtions. Because they, and not conditions, determine where they are on the Line, **they are able to choose their experiences.** This doesn't mean that every day is happy. What it does mean is that they are authors of their own lives and not merely characters in someone else's story. **They are creators of their life rather than helpless victims.**

PARENTING LOOKS DIFFERENT ABOVE AND BELOW THE LINE

Top 20 Parents know that things look different whether they are Above or Below the Line. Bottom 80 Parents are unaware that where they are on the Line causes them to see differently.

Let's consider how Jamie's mother sees him when she's Above or Below the Line:

He's a wonderful son who is loving and caring. She enjoys pleasing him and special moments they share together.

He's a brat who is selfish and doesn't listen. She yells at him which confuses him and damages their relationship.

Who's changed? Jamie hasn't really changed; he just **looks different** to mom when she's Below the Line.

Parents not only see their children or problems differently when they are Above or Below the Line, they also parent differently.

When we are operating as Bottom 80 Parents, we are not **'bad'**. It's just that our thinking, learning and communicating are not serving us well as we parent our children. Top 20 Parents strive to live ATL because they know how that affects their parenting abilities. Approaching parenting

"I didn't know how much my own negativity would show up in my daughter's behavior."

–A Parent

from an ATL perspective helps us think, learn and communicate more effectively.

Above the Line Parent	Below the Line Parent
• Has a positive view of child.	• Has a negative view of child.
• Accepts the behavior of child as part of his development.	• Doesn't understand child's behavior as part of his development.
• Has empathy toward child.	• Has no empathy for child.
• Is patient and understanding.	• Is angry and resentful.
• Believes parenting involves teaching when mistakes occur.	• Believes child should be punished for mistakes.
• Works with child's stage of development and temperament instead of against it.	• Works against child's stage of development and temperament instead of with it.
• Keeps end goals of parenting in mind.	• Has no end goal in mind.

TAKING RESPONSIBILITY FOR OUR LIVES

As parents, how do we answer the question: Are our children causing us to dip BTL? Bottom 80s would say 'yes'. They believe it's the outside conditions (the child's behavior) that makes them go Below. Top 20s would say 'no'. They know it's their own state of mind and not their children that's causing them to go Below.

Are Top 20 Parents problem free? No. Their cars break down, the baby throws up on the new rug, their credit cards get stolen and their plumbing pipes get clogged. It's not that they don't have problems, but they approach problems with a state of mind that is in their Best Interest.

Do Top 20 Parents solve all their problems? No. Some health or financial problems may last forever, but they approach these situations with a state of mind that helps them live with the problems more effectively. Furthermore, because they're not making poor decisions BTL, they avoid some messes that Bottom 80s create.

All parents have the potential to become Top 20 Parents and raise Top 20 Kids. All families can have more enjoyable relationships and experiences if they are more attuned to their Line by being aware of their Invitations and Indicators and how to use Submarines and Trampolines.

INVITATIONS

Invitations are those conditions we experience as parents that make it likely for us to dip Below the Line. Maybe it's a child refusing to eat breakfast, overdue rent, health issues or relationship troubles. Maybe it's a remark from a relative about how we parent. Maybe it's being perpetually fatigued from not getting enough sleep. Maybe it's a broken dishwasher, a grumpy cashier at the grocery store or an angry driver who cuts us off in traffic. Invitations for a child include being tired or hungry, frustration over toys or not getting enough physical activity.

When we experience these conditions, we are invited to attend a Below the Line party. They ask us to RSVP. We can either respond by going Below or declining the invitation and staying Above. Remember, whenever we attend a BTL party, we BYON (Bring Your Own Negativity) which we will share with others.

Top 20s know this is their choice. Bottom 80s believe the conditions make them go to the BTL party. However we decide to RSVP, it will make all the difference in the world.

INDICATORS

Indicators are the feelings we have or behaviors we exhibit when we're Below the Line. They tell us that our thinking is not serving us well.

Sample Child Indicators:

> **Feelings:** irritable, frustrated, angry, sad, fear
> **Behaviors:** whining, crying, hitting, withdawing, uncooperative

Some of these might also be Indicators of parents.

Sample Parent Indicators:

> **Feelings:** resentful, tired, impatient, inadequate, worry
> **Behaviors:** punishing, sarcasm, yelling, withholding love

Imagine how difficult life can be for people to live together in harmony without understanding or communicating about Indicators. A child might get very confused when a parent's behavior constantly changes from ATL to BTL. Our children might think adults have dangerous and scary multiple personalities instead of one reliable personality that can be trusted with some predictability. What's little Jamie thinking when he asks for cookies twice and gets two very different reactions from his mom?

Top 20 Parents let their children know that when they are upset about life they aren't upset with them. Often children are caught in the middle of how **we** are reacting to events. Young children don't choose to live BTL with us, but they will find themselves there a lot if we are not careful.

TRAMPOLINES

The importance of Invitations and Indicators is that they help us be aware of where we are on our Line. They let us know when we're Below. Now what? What can we do if we discover that we're BTL?

Bottom 80s wait passively for their situation to improve. Top 20s, however, know that just as certain experiences are invitations to go BTL, they can create their own **Trampoline** experiences that **help them change their perspective and bounce back Above the Line.**

Examples of Trampolines include the following activities:

- Spending quiet time alone
- Talking to a trusted friend
- Exercising, going for a walk
- Helping someone in need
- Focusing on the present, not the problem

- Enjoying a hobby activity
- Listening to music
- Praying or meditating
- Writing in a journal to sort thoughts
- Thinking of a loved one or enjoyable memory or place

We may be in a situation, such as a meeting or social gathering, where we can't leave to get exercise or special alone time listening to music or enjoying a hobby. However, we can improve our thinking at these times by simply changing our perspective or being grateful for what we have. A father whose entire body was confined in a narrow cylinder during an MRI exam recalled special times with his young children. By changing his perspective and being grateful for meaningful moments from his past, he trampolined to a more enjoyable experience.

Drugs, alcohol or excessive eating or spending would not be useful Trampolines. These just keep us BTL or draw us down further. If clinical depression is keeping someone BTL, then getting help from a doctor is an appropriate Trampoline.

Trampolines are a way of taking care of ourselves. This is crucial in our parenting role because children's needs are best met by parents whose needs are met. Furthermore, helping our children discover their own Trampolines is a way of helping them take care of themselves.

Examples of Trampolines for young children might be:

- Taking a nap
- Snuggling a special stuffed toy
- Reading a book with a caregiver
- Sensory play such as sand play, playdough, or a warm bath

As many of these activities imply, often the quickest way to get unstuck from the clutches of BTL thinking is to think about something else for awhile. Top 20 parents help their children can be unstuck from a bad mood or negative thoughts by redirecting them to a new activity.

SUBMARINES

Being BTL can be like sinking under water without oxygen. The flailing of our arms and legs can hurt ourselves or someone close to us. Consequently, when Top 20s sink BTL, they go in a Submarine.

When we are BTL, we may not realistically be able to get back Above immediately. A **Submarine** is a metaphor for protecting ourselves and others while we are Below. It's **a way of containing our negativity and maintaining our dignity so we don't create a bigger mess while we are visiting Below.**

Another function of the Submarine is to sound the alarm. We can alert others that we are BTL and are taking ourselves out of the action for the time being. We can let others know that they are not the reason for our anger, frustration or sadness. Imagine the different experience Jamie and his mother would have had if she would have said, "Honey, mommy's worried about something at work. I'm a little upset now but it has nothing to do with you. You're very special and I love you very much." Those few words would have prevented her negativity from being dumped onto her son.

11

In summary, being in a Submarine keeps our negative BTL energy in check so we don't pass it on and make a bigger mess. It gives us time to get our attitude adjusted so we can put our energy into getting ATL where our thinking, learning and communicating serve us well and will help us solve our problems in ways that will be in our Best Interest.

Remember, Submarines only have limited amounts of oxygen. Tempting as it might sometimes be, we cannot stay away from life forever. Sooner or later, we must resurface.

DEVELOPMENTAL NEWS FLASH!!!

• **Young children are concrete learners.** They understand best about things they can see and touch. Thinking Above and Below an imaginary line is too abstract for young children. By drawing or role playing we can help them understand this abstract concept over time. For example, use drawings of sad or happy faces to talk about moods with young children or a toy submarine during bath time to show how one can be protected from the water.

• **Young children have limited emotional awareness.** They initially have a very limited emotional vocabulary. They may not be able to communicate their negative feelings to us any other way than acting them out. We can teach them more about their emotions, the causes of their moods, their Invitations and Indicators. Giving them the labels for emotions like frustration, worry, fear and jealousy can help a child be more self aware. Acting out some scenarios of how a child might act ATL and BTL (for example, dropping a delicious ice cream cone or breaking a toy) will help them see themselves in sharper focus and understand the emotions of others.

Children can begin to understand the difference between good days and bad days or good experiences and bad experiences. They can be led to see the cause and effect of how moods can affect the bigger picture of their day.

• **Young children are easily distractible.** When thinking about changing moods, young kids have something in their favor. Infants and toddlers will generally respond quickly to something new being introduced. They have the ability to move away from bothersome situations and refocus on something else. Parents can help them to stop focusing on whatever is putting them BTL by distracting and redirecting them with a new activity, experience or object.

Preschoolers, however, are not as easily distracted. Preschoolers can be led to new activities or moods when they can be convinced it's in their Best Interest.

It may take a little more than simply showing them something new. Helpful strategies include:

- Giving them a new focus (a special toy, a snack, bubbles) that we know is a favorite.
- Showing them that they are out of step with the rest of the group: "Everyone else is cleaning up so we can go outside to play."
- Connecting how being ATL or BTL is affecting their experience: "When you push your friend, he doesn't want to play with you anymore."

OUR BEST INTEREST IS OUR KID'S BEST INTEREST

We have seen how the concept of Above and Below the Line can be applied to decision making. It can also be applied to relationship making. Family relationships are meant to last a long time and weather many things. Think of a car about to make a long trip. Which car would you trust to make the long haul: a well-serviced car that is repaired and maintained as needed or a car with flat tires, faulty breaks and a blinking oil light that has been ignored?

An ATL parent is like the well-serviced car ready to handle a long journey. A parent who is BTL is like the car that will let us down when it encounters bumps in the road. Understanding this concept can help us be aware when our thinking, learning and communicating is serving us well and when they need to be 'repaired'.

As parents, it's in our Best Interest and the Best Interest of our children to take care of ourselves. Remember, **children's needs are best met by parents whose needs are met.** We are helping the people we live with when we help ourselves live Above the Line.

THE POWER TO CHOOSE

As our understanding of this concept deepens, we will more quickly detect when we are BTL and more quickly get back ATL. **As we accept greater responsibility for our life, we will be more aware of the power we have to determine our experience regardless of the circumstances.** This awareness gives us the power to go in the direction we truly wish to go and accomplish our parenting goals. We know that when we are ATL we are better able to solve problems with greater wisdom and handle the daily hits and negative events that occur in all families.

For Parents to Do:

1. What are your typical Invitations and Indicators? How do they affect the outcome of your day?

2. Look for patterns and reasons for when you are ATL and BTL. Does what you observe prompt you to make any changes?

3. What Trampolines can you use to move Above the Line?

4. How can you use a Submarine when you are Below the Line?

To Do with Your Child:

1. Observe for your child's Invitations and Indicators.

2. Is your child finding Trampolines that work? How can you help your child with Trampolines that get her ATL?

3. Observe for patterns and reasons for your child being ATL or BTL. Does what you observe prompt you to make any changes?

4. Create an Above and Below the Line chart with moveable pictures of each family member. Each day each person can mark where he is on the Line by placing his picture at that spot.

CHAPTER 3

The Frame
What You SEE Is What You GET

"Things are not what they seem."
—Henry Wadsworth Longfellow

Parents and their three-year-olds were busy in the classroom during a planned playtime. Suddenly screaming and crying caught everyone's attention. Across the room, Daniel had Caitlyn in a head lock. Several parents rushed to rescue Caitlyn from Daniel's grip. Angrily, Daniel's mother, Susan, picked her son up and, with his legs dangling, held him in front of her face, "What is wrong with you, Daniel? Use your words. You just don't listen!" With tears in his eyes, Daniel kicked his mother.

Sensing both anger and embarrassment in Susan and Daniel, the parenting instructor suggested they accompany her to the hall where they could calm down and talk. Daniel sat on a bench with his head hanging as Susan demanded to know why his behavior was so bad. The instructor intervened and got to the root of the scuffle by asking him what he was trying to do by getting Caitlyn in a headlock. He lifted his head and very bravely said, "I was trying to get Caitlyn to listen to me. I did use my words but she wouldn't listen to me. I figured out how we could both be first, but she wouldn't listen to me!"

Suddenly Susan was able to see her son in a new way. Even though Daniel's behavior needed to be addressed, his mother was able to understand his actions. Although she didn't know it at the time, Susan was using the Frame to see her son differently.

Both Top 20s and Bottom 80s want to get what's important to them. The difference, however, is that Top 20s know what to do when they are not getting what's important. They understand and use the Frame.

WHAT IS THE FRAME?

The Frame is an important tool for a successful journey in life. It helps us be aware of **the connection between how we see and the results we get.**

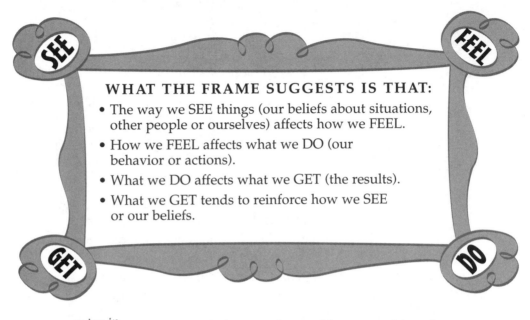

WHAT THE FRAME SUGGESTS IS THAT:

- The way we SEE things (our beliefs about situations, other people or ourselves) affects how we FEEL.
- How we FEEL affects what we DO (our behavior or actions).
- What we DO affects what we GET (the results).
- What we GET tends to reinforce how we SEE or our beliefs.

"I use the Frame everyday in some kind of situation."

–A Mom

The Frame helps us solve problems, see things in a different way, change our responses and get what's important to us. As such, it is important for three reasons:

    1. Human beings operate with a Frame in every situation. Whereas Top 20s are aware of this, Bottom 80s are usually clueless about the Frame and its impact on their lives.

2. It's a tool for change when we are **not** getting what's important to us.

3. It can help us see differently when things cannot be changed.

REFRAMING

If we are getting what we want to be getting, if we are getting what is important to us, then we should keep doing what we are doing, feeling what we are feeling, and seeing it how we are seeing it. But if we are not getting what we want to be getting, we need to see differently. The act of **seeing** differently can be called **Reframing.** By Reframing we will get a different perspective, point of view, attitude or approach. Being able to see in a new light can be a powerful tool for creating more satisfying experiences in our life.

Let's look at the example of a child screaming and crying in front of the candy display at a store. The way we see this child will likely make a difference in the results we get.

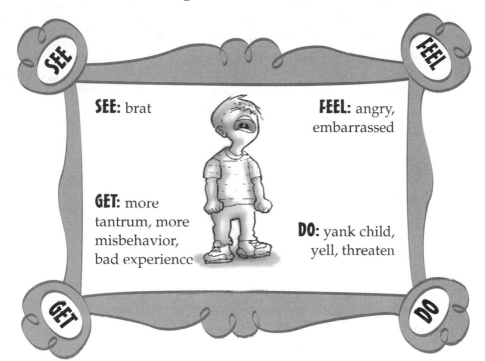

SEE: brat

FEEL: angry, embarrassed

GET: more tantrum, more misbehavior, bad experience

DO: yank child, yell, threaten

Let's Reframe the same child.

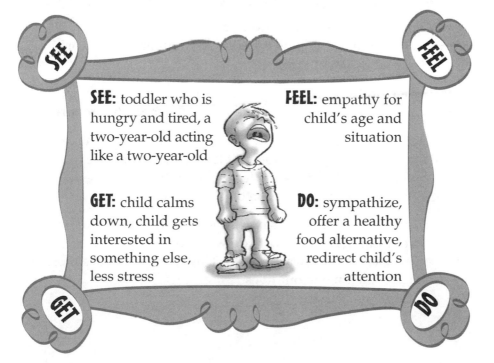

SEE: toddler who is hungry and tired, a two-year-old acting like a two-year-old

FEEL: empathy for child's age and situation

GET: child calms down, child gets interested in something else, less stress

DO: sympathize, offer a healthy food alternative, redirect child's attention

BOTTOM 80s AND THE FRAME

Bottom 80s don't realize they are operating with a Frame and remain relatively close-minded to solutions that might bring about improvement. Unaware of how their seeing impacts the outcome, they don't change the cycle that causes an event to happen over and over again. Consequently nothing changes. Bottom 80s keep getting undesirable results. They stay **stuck in yuck.**

Parenting offers many opportunities for getting stuck. For example, not knowing that children behave the way they do because of development and temperament may cause us to see them in a negative way. We may feel badly about a situation but don't know how to make changes. If we cannot SEE in a different way, we will continue to FEEL the same way, DO the same things and GET undesired results. The frustration caused by making no headway in situations we want to change leads us to get 'stuck'. As we sink deeper into 'yuck', we often pull others along with us.

"Let's not forget that the little emotions are the great captains of our lives and we obey them without realizing it."

—Vincent Van Gogh

BOTTOM 80 REACTIONS TO UNDESIRABLE RESULTS

We all experience times when we don't get what we want. Top 20 thinking and Bottom 80 thinking differ in these situations. Bottom 80s typically respond in one of three ways:

1. They **change nothing:** They continue to see the situation the way they always have. They behave the same way but **expect** different results.

   Susan expected Daniel's behavior to change. However, if she continued to see Daniel as a bully who wouldn't listen, she'd continue to feel angry and frustrated and use ineffective discipline strategies. As a result, nothing would change. She'd be stuck in yuck.

   Seeing, feeling and doing the same thing but expecting different results is a form of insanity. If we always do what we've always done, we'll always get what we've always gotten. This is an experience most of us have had at some time in our lives.

2. They **change what they do:** It makes sense that by changing their behavior they will get different results. However, by **only** changing what they do, Bottom 80s don't bring about the big change they desire.

Susan could refrain from picking him up to avoid being kicked. However, if she still sees him as a bully and remains angry, she may avoid being kicked but won't discover what she needs to understand to bring about big change in his behavior.

Bottom 80s believe that the DO corner is the most powerful part of the Frame. It seems that taking action is the best way to affect change. In fact, we are often advised to do just that: "If I were you, I'd do....What you should do is....You're not doing it right." But without understanding the cause and effect relationship between the other corners of the Frame, focusing on the DO corner alone will not bring about beneficial results.

> "It is a painful thing to look at your own trouble and know that you yourself and no one else has made it."
>
> –Sophocles

3. They **blame** someone else or conditions for the bad results they're getting. This is the most common response Bottom 80s make when they are not getting the results they desire. By blaming, Bottom 80s transfer their power to make a difference to whomever or whatever they are blaming. Consequently, they become a powerless victim and stay stuck in yuck.

Think of a child having a tantrum in front of the candy display. Not realizing that he is hungry and should be home napping, his mother could blame him or the store manager for putting the candy at eye level. If so, this same situation would likely happen again in the future. Blame would prevent her from realizing the power she has to help herself and her son better navigate this situation.

TOP 20 RESPONSES TO UNDESIRABLE RESULTS

When Top 20s experience not getting the results they want to be getting, they respond with two powerful and interconnected strategies.

1. They are **curious:** Top 20s never give up power to make a difference in their lives by blaming. Rather, they expand their power by being curious and seeking more information that will be useful in problem solving. Curiosity results in asking: "How can I see this person... situation...myself differently?"

2. They **reframe what they see:** Top 20s know that the most powerful corner of the Frame is SEE. A change in seeing gives them the potential for big changes. By reframing we keep an open mind and listen to our children and others to understand what might otherwise be missed. Top 20s know that if they can **see** things differently, they will eventually **get** different results.

"When we learned in class that whatever children do at the time is right for them at that particular moment, I suddenly was able to see differently and reframe my son's behavior."

–A Dad

PARADIGM SHIFTS

Paradigms are our patterned or habitual way of seeing or thinking. Susan had a patterned way of seeing her son as a bully. A paradigm shift (reframing) occurs when we change how we see something.

What can parents do to reframe and get a new, more effective perspective on their children, situations or conditions? Let's consider four ways to shift our paradigms and improve our sight where we might have been previously blind.

1. **Create a Crisis.** Nothing is more effective than a crisis in bringing about paradigm shifts that result in our seeing something differently. Many of us have to get to this point before we are willing to reframe our life. Think of 9/11. Don't we see many things differently because of that national crisis? We even see the numbers 9/11 differently. But do we really want to get to a crisis every time change needs to happen in our family? We can use three painless ways to bring about reframing.

2. **Ask Others How They See It.** Another way to reframe and see more is to ask someone else how he sees the situation. No two people see anything exactly alike. That is why it is so valuable to share parenting with a spouse, relative, mentor or friend. Parenting can be lonely and isolating. If we have been carrying the load of parenting virtually alone, others can help us see situations from a new perspective. In such situations it's wise to ask someone who we think might see it differently rather than someone who will agree with us.

3. **Change Roles.** We will change how we see if we change roles. How does the situation look to a child? We can use our own memories as a youngster to empathize with our child and reframe the situation through our child's perspective.

"Intelligence also encompasses flexibility, the ability to see issues from a variety of viewpoints."

–Robert J. Sternberg

4. Say 'Maybe'. Have you ever noticed trees growing out of rock? It actually happens. They can't grow out of solid rock but huge trees can grow where there's a crack in a rock.

Sometimes our opinions and judgments can be solid as a rock and prevent us from seeing differently. Putting 'maybe' before our opinions and judgments, especially our more negative statements about our children, leaves room for new possibilities. If we change our judgement from "He's being a brat" to "Maybe he's being a brat," we may see other reasons why he's behaving this way. The difference in this statement may seem subtle, but 'Maybe' allows the potential for change by allowing us to see new possibilities.

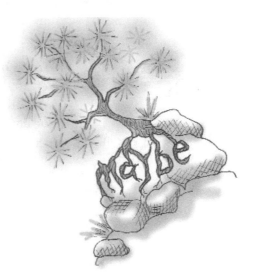

THREE RIGHTS

Have you ever noticed how important it is for people to be right? Sometimes being right matters more than being effective or getting what's really important to us. When that happens, our need to be right can keep us from getting the results we want.

Let's look at three different ways of thinking about being right that are likely to pop up when we're not getting what we want to be getting.

R = R

1. When we think we are Right, we're Right. In this view of being right, there are no other possibilities or options. There is no other way of seeing it. This is a Bottom 80 way of being right because it leads directly to blame. If we're not getting what's important to us and we think we're right, then someone or something else must be wrong. Since we're right, we can just blame someone else. In blaming, we give up power to make a difference and stay Stuck in Yuck. Doesn't that sound like a Bottom 80 experience?

> "Don't expect children to behave under circumstances that are not child-oriented."
> –Magda Gerber

What are the implications for parenting? Parents can mistakenly think they are right when they label a child's behavior, such as spilling juice or throwing food on the floor, as naughty or intentional. In truth, these behaviors in early childhood are most often rooted in developmental issues. However, because these parents believe they are right in labeling their child a behavior problem, they are no longer curious about solutions. Their opinions about their child are set.

21

Once seen through the Frame as a behavior problem, the child remains a behavior problem. Parents who think they are right in this judgment wait for their child to change. This waiting keeps them from searching for alternative solutions. These parents, feeling powerless, will be heard saying, "I give up. I don't know what to do about this behavior."

R=W

2. When we think we're Right, we're aware that we might be Wrong but just haven't discovered what we're Wrong about yet. Strange as it may seem, this is a Top 20 way of thinking. Why? If we think we might be wrong, we won't blame someone else. Because it prevents blame and leads to curiosity, we will see something more or differently and create a Top 20 experience.

In parenting, we might expect that we should be right because we are the parent or the adult. Many parents have been raised to believe that the parent is always right and children are to do as they are told "because I say so!" Top 20 parents embrace a different way of thinking. Instead of blaming or feeling weakened in their role as parents, they find strength and authority in being able to admit that they don't know everything. Their authority comes from how they use the Frame.

Consider a parent who thought he was right in punishing his two-year-old daughter for not sharing her toys with other children. He became curious when the punishments were not working. Once he gained more knowledge about child development, he realized that he was wrong to expect a two-year-old child to always share.

R=R+

3. When we think we're Right, we are Right, but there's always something more that we're not seeing. This is another Top 20 way of thinking. Top 20s know they never see anything (other people, a situation, even themselves) exactly the way it is. They are curious to get more information because they know that they may not have all the puzzle pieces. They acknowledge that the situations they are encountering might be misleading or confusing. Suspecting that they might be missing something, they remain curious and open to information that helps them see more or differently.

Let's look at an example of how this applies to parenting. When a child is picked up from daycare, she tantrums right in the doorway and breaks her baby brother's toy. The parent is right in

"Fred was screaming at a high pitch upstairs. My usual reaction would have been to scream back, 'Didn't I tell you not to scream!' This time I looked for more information and went upstairs to see why he was screaming. Fred, in an effort to dress himself, had layered so many clothes on himself, he could hardly move. It was as if he was in a strait jacket. I avoided a lot of anger and felt only sympathy. He was only screaming for help."

—A Mom

thinking that breaking her sibling's toy is unsatisfactory behavior, but is curious to find out more information. In checking with the daycare provider, the parent discovers that the little girl missed her nap, lost her beloved show-and-tell item on the field trip and seems to be coming down with a cold. More information results in the parent seeing her daughter differently and responding differently to her daughter's behaviors.

Top 20 parents can also think they are right. However, before making final decisions or judgments, they actively look for more information. They use the power of the Frame to make positive changes by looking at situations, people or events differently.

TWO PATHS

In every situation in our life we can take one of two paths. The more we are aware of these possibilities, the more likely we will choose the Top 20 path.

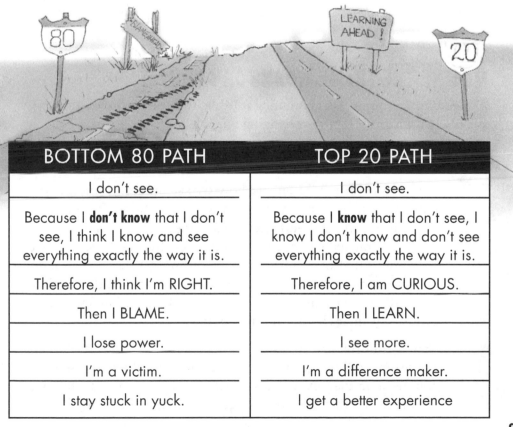

BOTTOM 80 PATH	TOP 20 PATH
I don't see.	I don't see.
Because I **don't know** that I don't see, I think I know and see everything exactly the way it is.	Because I **know** that I don't see, I know I don't know and don't see everything exactly the way it is.
Therefore, I think I'm RIGHT.	Therefore, I am CURIOUS.
Then I BLAME.	Then I LEARN.
I lose power.	I see more.
I'm a victim.	I'm a difference maker.
I stay stuck in yuck.	I get a better experience

DEVELOPMENTAL NEWS FLASH!!!

Children can't make use of the Frame until they have the cognitive ability to put themselves in someone else's place. Two developmental factors get in the way.

• **Young children are concrete learners.** They think concretely and understand best about things they can see and feel. They are new to abstract thinking and will have trouble understanding the Frame concept. Nevertheless, young children can be challenged to reach for abstract thinking. Making learning moments out of their concrete experiences will help children become aware of how the Frame guides their feelings, actions and outcomes. For example, pointing out how feeling angry and then breaking a friend's toy can lead to the end of a friendship will be a concrete way to give insight to the elements of the Frame.

• **Young children are egocentric.** Young children can naturally see only one perspective — their own. However, they are ready to have discussions introducing other peoples' points of view. We can use our child's own personal experiences to understand the perspectives of others. For example, we can talk about how actions are viewed by others ("Grandma liked it when you said thank you.") and how people experiencing the same situation can feel differently ("You enjoyed seeing the animals at the zoo, but Peter was afraid of the lions.") In this way, we are developing in our child's awareness that other people have perspectives and feelings that may be different.

MAKING THE FRAME WORK FOR FAMILIES

By regularly reframing our parenting role, we will see ourselves differently as our children grow. Perhaps changing our role from 'protector' to 'caregiver' or from 'disciplinarian' to 'teacher' will be enough to change our feelings, actions and outcomes.

How we see our children and how we see ourselves affects our parenting choices and the outcomes of our actions. Our views of our children affect their own views of themselves. If we see a child as a lazy brat, as wild or as a whiner, that child will also come to see himself that way and behave accordingly. When we, as parents, reframe our views of our children, we allow our children a chance to see themselves differently. That affects their self image and, ultimately, their choices and behavior.

Young children get their self image largely from the adults who are closest to them, spend the most time with them and see and comment on their every move each day. Our comments tell our children who they are. Self image guides their emerging characters, like a trellis that helps a plant to grow tall and strong. When children are told that they are irritating, messy, stupid, clumsy or mean, they will grow that way. When children are told they are capable, precious, helpful or kind, they will grow and flourish in that direction. If we can use the Frame to **see the potential of our children,** then the by-product is that **our children will see themselves as full of potential.**

For Parents to Do:

1. Recall how your parents saw or framed you as a child. Were you seen correctly? How did that affect your view of yourself?

2. Consider one of your child's most irritating behaviors. How do you see it? How do you feel about it? What do you do about this? What results are you getting? Look for a new way to see and understand those behaviors.

To Do with Your Child:

Since children cannot make use of the Frame until they have the cognitive ability to put themselves in someone else's place, you can help your child start recognizing the feelings of others by:

1. Looking at faces, books or magazines and discussing emotions with your child.

2. Showing the cause and effect relationship that can exist between not getting what you want because of behavior: "You wanted her to play with you, but when you hit her she ran away."

3. Sharing the perspectives of other people and explaining how actions can be misunderstood: "When you yelled in excitement, Gina got scared and cried. Gina saw your face and hand movements as you being angry with her, even if you didn't mean it that way."

CHAPTER 4

The Big Picture
The WHY's of Child Behavior

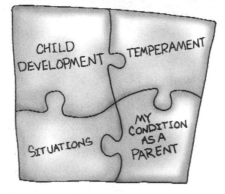

"When you think about it, there are so many puzzle pieces. How could you figure your child out with only one puzzle piece?"

–A Parent

Isabel picked up her son from daycare before making a quick stop at the grocery store. As they dashed toward the long check out lines, Billy saw a display of his favorite cereal and demanded a box to take home. Although Isabel told him there was a full box at home, Billy had a screaming tantrum in the busy store. The more she tried to talk to her son the louder he screamed. She couldn't think straight. Embarrassed, Isabel bought the cereal to quiet him and get out of the store. Angry at her son and herself, Isabel saw Billy as a behavior problem and herself as a failure.

THE WHY'S OF CHILD BEHAVIOR

Many factors, issues and perspectives contribute to the Big Picture of a child's behavior. However, when the pressure is on in day-to-day parenting, it's hard to see the Big Picture and think straight. Although we may think we understand a child's behavior from one specific incident, we often miss the full scope and many details of the total picture.

Our children and their behaviors are like challenging puzzles. How much could we tell about a puzzle if we only had one small piece? When looking at child behavior, we can't assume that one puzzle piece will give us all the information we need. We need to collect more information if we are to understand WHY a child behaves a certain way. Anger doesn't help Isabel at the grocery store. Curiosity would. She needs to ask: "Why did my child behave that way?"

Human behavior always has a reason behind it. We are motivated to act a certain way because there is something we wish to accomplish. To view any behavior as a simple act without the reasoning behind it can be futile. Seeing several motivational pieces of a child's behavior helps a parent see the Big Picture more quickly and find a more effective response to a child's behavior.

To have a clear sense of the Big Picture regarding child behavior we need to consider four distinct puzzle pieces:

CHILD DEVELOPMENT   TEMPERAMENT   SITUATIONS   MY CONDITION AS A PARENT

Being aware of how these critical pieces fit together will help us respond more effectively to our children.

CHILD DEVELOPMENT

Development is the predictable path taken by growing children. Children are wired for development. Because it takes a lot of work and persistence to learn new things, no one would bother if there wasn't a biological urge to progress.

All children go through the same stages of development in roughly the same order. Each stage has its own unique child behaviors that may be problematic and frustrating. Children will develop at their own pace, no matter what we as parents might wish. In other words, **the voice of their development is louder than our parent voice.**

Development means a child is changing every day. As we work on mastering one stage of development, our child is already moving on to the next. Just when child behavior may start to make sense, development can upset all the puzzle pieces causing us to start again.

Development is an important life long process and will be easier for children whose parents understand its different stages. By knowing what is **developmentally appropriate**, the characteristics and behaviors that are expected for children at certain ages, parents can better understand and manage their children's behavior. Knowing about developmental stages allows parents to predict a child's capabilities and limitations. This knowledge enables parents to have realistic goals and expectations for children.

Since Child Development is such an important puzzle piece, more can be learned about your ever-changing child from sources available in libraries and book stores.

Temperament is the package of social, emotional and physiological factors that nature bestows uniquely on each person. It is how we take in the world and respond to it.

Temperament traits include:

- Persistence
- Regularity
- Quality of mood
- Adaptability
- Approachability
- Intensity of reactions
- Activity level
- Sensory threshold
- Distractibility

These specific traits are neither good nor bad. It is not better to be one temperament or another. However, this unique bundle of traits gives each person strengths, weaknesses and much potential.

In becoming Top 20 Parents we need to know what each temperament trait means and recognize how temperament and child behavior are connected. (More about temperament and these traits will be covered in detail in Chapter 9.) For instance, a child jumping on the furniture might be linked to activity level or a child refusing to leave play and come when called might be linked to persistence. We must be able to take an additional step to connect behaviors that we see in a child to the temperament trait from which the behavior might stem.

Situations affect behavior. Some of the more obvious situations that can affect a child's behaviors are amount of sleep, hunger, time of day or being in unfamiliar surroundings. Health concerns, such as allergies, pain, infections and nutrition, can affect behavior for both children and parents. It is hard to concentrate on anything else when a situation is affecting a person's ability to cope and process information accurately.

Some situations that affect child behavior are not as obvious, such as being confined too long in a restrictive environment like a car seat, stroller or grocery cart or being over stimulated by a lot of group activity, bright lights or loud sounds. Adding understanding about how situations affect and influence behaviors to the other puzzle pieces is another step to completing the Big Picture of child behavior.

As we have seen in the chapter on Above and Below the Line, it is important to acknowledge that the condition of the parent is a puzzle piece in explaining why a child might be behaving in a certain way. The conditions of the parent may include mood, lack of sleep, response to the weather, family relationships, and physical and mental health. Other conditions might include past or present family relationships, stress from things such as a job, finances, neighborhood and safety issues, the opinions of others that undermine one's parenting or not getting one's needs met as a person. These conditions can often affect parenting attitudes, decisions and actions, shaping how we view and react to child behaviors.

"Children's needs are best met by parents whose needs are met."

–ECFE wisdom

WHAT TO DO ABOUT CHILD BEHAVIOR

Top 20 Parents first gather pertinent information about the puzzle pieces of child behavior before asking: "What can I do about a behavior?" With all the puzzle pieces in place, the Big Picture of child behavior becomes more clear. With clarity, we can devise a successful plan to solve challenging behaviors for both our child and ourselves.

Bottom 80 parents react. They quickly feel what the behavior means to them and act impulsively. **Top 20 parents respond.** They take time to think carefully about what the behavior means to all parties involved before choosing action. They more effectively solve behavior problems by pausing, thinking, making choices based on their values and then acting.

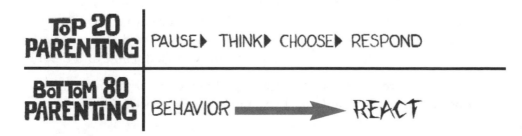

The Top 20 Parenting response tends to move towards a satisfactory solution to a problem while the Bottom 80 Parenting reaction tends to create a second problem worse than the first.

Let's consider an example. Sometimes parents report that when their baby or young toddler bites them, they quickly and impulsively hit the child. That's a Bottom 80 reaction. A Top 20 parental response would be to pause, think and choose the course of action. It would take into account developmental reasons for biting, such as teething, frustration, curiosity about oral sensation or attention seeking. Actions chosen might then be to say 'no' while showing the pain of the bite and giving the child something appropriate to chew on like a teething toy. Top 20 thinking would consider the developmental stages of a child and a Top 20 response would create opportunities for teaching instead of punishment.

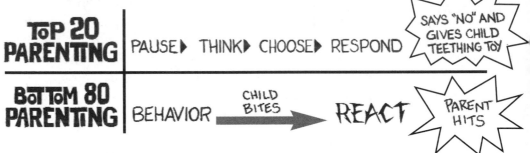

PUTTING ALL THE PIECES TOGETHER

Each of the four areas discussed in this chapter work together to create the Big Picture of our children's behaviors. None of the pieces can be omitted to get a true understanding of why a child is acting a certain way.

Having the correct information about the details of our own and our child's unique Big Picture is a part of Top 20 Parenting. If any specific issues or serious concerns emerge from reflecting on these questions, a need for professional expertise may be required. Consider talking to a doctor or other health professional for additional information or support.

Putting all the puzzle pieces together is like a pilot flying an airplane. Pilots need to know the end destination of a trip and variables that could cause problems along the way. They need to research weather conditions and the location of other planes, listen to feedback from air traffic controllers with different perspectives and be prepared to go with the air flow. Unthinking reactions to the unpredictable could be dangerous and take the pilot off course. Successful pilots are knowledgeable and flexible.

Top 20 Parents are like pilots. Parents need to take many factors into account in order to respond wisely and not react ineffectively. Parents flying in a Top 20 way have goals and destinations but also scan the Big Picture for clues about their children's temperament, development, situations and their own adult conditions. Top 20 Parents seek feedback from others and flexibly go with the flow of each day. Flexibility is not to be confused with being permissive. It does not mean changing goals for a child's whining demands, tantrums or whims. Top 20 Parenting observes for information that finds the best route to the end destination, successfully avoiding many problems along the way.

"Cierra would not get out of the car seat when we went to the grocery store. I finally realized the situation. These errands took place after my work when I was tired and so was she. When I learned that because of her temperament she needs to adjust to the situation and time of day, I found a strategy that really works. Now we stop and sit for a minute at the deli chairs just inside the doors of the grocery store and talk."

—**A Mother**

TIME FOR ACTION!

For Parents to Do:

1. What behaviors in your child do you see as challenging?

2. How do the following puzzle pieces affect your child's behavior:

   A. Child Development: How is development playing a part in the behavior you see?

   B. Temperament: Which of the temperament traits (p. 28) might be affecting your child's behavior?

   C. Situation: Is your child reacting to any of the following situations?

Time of day	Unfamiliar surroundings
Lack of sleep	Adult reactions to a behavior
Hunger	Confinement in a restrictive environment
Health concerns	Sensory overload

D. My Own Condition as a Parent:

- How does your temperament affect your behavior?
- What expectations do you have for your child? Are they realistic according to development, temperament or the situation your child is in?
- What conditions are affecting you as a parent?

Mood	Sleep	Weather
Family relationships	Self esteem	Physical health
Mental health	Personal stress	Unmet needs

3. What insights do you have now that you have considered these questions?

4. What can you do differently to parent more effectively?

To Do with Your Child:

Observe your child throughout an entire day.

1. What development factors affected your child's behaviors?

2. What temperament factors affected your child's behaviors?

3. How did the situation affect your child's behavior?

4. How does your condition as a parent affect your child's behavior?

CHAPTER 5

Emotional Intelligence
A New Formula for Success

"These are hard times for children, and so for parents. There has been a sea change in the nature of childhood over the last decade or two, one that makes it harder for children to learn the basic lessons of the human heart..."
–Daniel Goleman

The twenty-year high school reunion party drew a large alumni crowd. Many were surprised that one of their most successful peers was Ibrahim. Never one for tests or grades, Ibrahim had even repeated a few tough academic courses. Those not surprised by his success were the teachers who had recognized and encouraged other strengths in him, namely his people skills and reliability. Now president of a computer repair company, Ibrahim manages a group of highly skilled employees, most of whom he has retained for many years. He has loyal customers who pass on to others the special service they receive at his company.

How do we know who will succeed and who will fail in life? In the past we have typically relied on academic performance and IQ tests to predict success: **High IQ = Success.** Although this is a strong belief held by many today, research has revealed that IQ is a poor predictor of life success.

In his book *Emotional Intelligence*, psychologist Daniel Goleman contributed to the discussion about measuring, predicting and teaching success by including the role of emotions as a factor of success: **Success = Emotional Quotient x Intellegence Quotient.** While IQ measures the ability to learn facts and figures, **EQ represents the ability to get along in the world by managing self and relating well to others.** "How we do in life," claims Goleman, "is determined by both–it is not just IQ, but emotional intelligence that matters."[2]

The balance of IQ and EQ in our lives can be compared to the wheels of a bicycle. The back wheel represents our IQ and the front wheel EQ. The back wheel drives the bike and the front wheel steers the bike. It is this front

wheel over which we have control when we grab the handle bars. By taking control, we can steer our life in the direction we want to go.

Let's consider two examples of the formula S = IQ x EQ:

Example 1: Sally was bright (IQ = 8), got A's in her classes, and had her hand up all the time in class. Being arrogant and boastful, she had few friends. Sally lacked self-awareness and people skills (EQ = 2). Her success total was only 16. If Sally could have increased her EQ, she might have improved her 'ride' through life.

$8 \times 2 = 16$

$5 \times 8 = 40$

Example 2: Meanwhile, behind Sally sat Ibrahim. He had average brainpower (IQ = 5) and struggled to get B's and C's. He was dependable, trustworthy and brought out the best in others (EQ = 8). His success total was 40, more than double that of Sally's. No nonder Ibrahim was successful with his employees and customers.

"People who succeed...are those who have managed to acquire, develop, and apply a full range of intellectual skills, rather than merely relying on the inert intelligence that schools so value."

–Robert Sternberg

COMPONENTS OF EMOTIONAL INTELLIGENCE

As described by Daniel Goleman, Emotional Intelligence, an expanded model of intelligence that puts emotions at the center of an aptitude for living, is comprised of five defining components:

1. **Recognizing one's own feelings:** As Socrates declared, "Know thyself". This self-awareness means understanding and monitoring moods and feelings. Control and confidence comes from these insights about oneself.

2. **Managing impulses and emotions:** We may have little control as to when an impulse occurs or what emotion will pop up at any given time, but we can manage how long an emotion will last and whether to act on an impulse. The goal is balance, not emotional suppression, with feelings that are proportionate or appropriate to a situation.

3. **Motivating oneself in the face of frustrations:** Enthusiasm, persistence, optimism and confidence are needed to achieve a goal and meet challenges through effort and control of impulses.

4. **Reading the feelings of others:** To have empathy and to know the emotions of others one must read the nonverbal cues, gestures, facial expressions, voice tones and inflections of others.

5. **Handling relationships well:** Interpersonal skills build on self-control of one's own emotions and impulses, empathy and attunement to oth-

ers, as well as the use of strategies like patience, argument or humor. People who have these leadership abilities are effective.[3]

Since this discussion is so important for Top 20 Parents who want to raise Top 20 Kids, EQ and character development are included in the next chapter and Appendix A: Star Qualities Activities.

THE ROLE THAT TEMPERAMENT PLAYS

Some emotional patterns and responses are part of a person's temperament, the genes of behavior that nature gives us. Temperament contributes to how quickly an emotion occurs, how intense it becomes and how long it lasts. But these emotional patterns can be changed and new ways can be learned. A shy child can become more outgoing. Persistence can be increased. Negative first responses can be moderated. A parent's response to a child's temperament traits and a child's own growing EQ skills can help to create temperament changes.

"Temperament is not destiny."
–Daniel Goleman

WHAT DOES EQ LOOK LIKE?

There are some reliable indicators that a person has low or high emotional intelligence.

Indicators of Low EQ	Indicators of High EQ
• inability to read nonverbal clues	• expressing feelings clearly and directly without fear
• inability to express facial emotions or talk about feelings	• reading nonverbal communication
• misunderstanding personal space	• balancing feelings with reason, logic and reality
• misuse of speech to communicate	• feeling empowered and motivated
• withdrawal	• optimistically expecting success
• anxiety and depression	• having empathy and interest in others
• aggression, acting out and impulsivity	• being well-behaved in school
• not taking responsibility for feelings	• learning more effectively
• low self-esteem	
• disrespect and judgment of others	

More than ever it seems children of all backgrounds, ethnicities and economic levels are at risk for low EQ. In young children low EQ might show itself in these ways:

"While any of these problems in isolation raises no eyebrows, taken as a group they are barometers of a sea change, a new kind of toxicity seeping into and poisoning the very experience of childhood, signifying sweeping deficits in emotional competences."

–Daniel Goleman

- not knowing how to join into games and groups,
- awkward social communication and touching,
- not understanding the cause and effect of social situations,
- problems in attending and focusing to instruction and learning.

In children high EQ would be evident in these ways:

- the ability to enter play and group situations
- the ability to calm distressing emotions in others
- being socially skilled with friends

DEVELOPMENTAL NEWS FLASH!!!

• **Young children are emotionally immature.** All young children have strong negative emotions that they are unequipped to communicate and will often 'act out' with misbehavior. Young children have not had enough life experiences to learn many EQ skills. In looking for EQ growth in young children, the limitations of their development must not be held against them. A parent can use a child's emotional experiences as teachable moments to develop EQ skills.

• **Young children have limited emotional awareness.** Young children initially have a very limited emotional vocabulary. They may not be aware of or able to label the myriad emotions they are experiencing. By narrating the emotional events that occur and giving labels for feelings like surprise, anxiety and anger, parents can help a child become more self aware.

• **The impulse control areas of the brain are not yet mature.** Young children will act before they think. It is hard for them to wait. The areas of the brain that control impulses and responses are not fully developed until twenty years of age or later.

• **The cause and effect of emotional situations and relationships is not well understood.** The cognitive development of young children is a work in progress. A child is not able to consistently understand, recognize or analyze how behaviors affect others. Even if aware, a young child may not be able to make the changes needed to create new patterns of behavior without the coaching of a patient parent.

• **Empathy develops over time through many experiences.** Infants cry when they hear other babies cry. By year one, young toddlers may try to comfort others. A one-year-old may be confused about what to do about the emotions of others, rubbing her own head if another child is hurt. Two-year-olds become increasingly skilled at reading nonverbal cues. They can interpret the emotional meaning of facial expressions and gestures. Some children may be approaching the teen years before feeling empathy for the larger world.

EQ AND TOP 20 PARENTING

Emotional Intelligence is important to family life and parenting. High EQ helps parents cope well with the ups and downs of family life. They can also help their children develop Emotional Intelligence. Parents who lack EQ have trouble managing family situations. Negative emotions can destroy their effectiveness as parents. For example, a mother having a bad day with her children in a supermarket may undergo what amounts to an emotional hijacking if a jar of mayonnaise breaks on the floor. Her emotions may take over her thinking brain and run away with it. A rough day can cumulatively feed upon itself until the mother's negative emotions are directed at the children and her own health is affected.

> "Thus someone who has had a hard day at work is especially vulnerable to becoming enraged later at home by something [like] the kids being too noisy or messy...that under other circumstances would not be powerful enough to trigger an emotional hijacking."
>
> –Daniel Goleman

EMOTIONAL COACHING

Research shows that some emotional problems of teen years can be prevented by giving younger children EQ tools. Because family life is the first school of emotions for young children, John Gottman, in *The Heart of Parenting: Raising an Emotionally Intelligent Child,* believes parents have many opportunities to be an emotional coach, to guide their children through the confusing world of emotion by teaching "their kids how to regulate their feelings, find appropriate outlets, and solve problems."[4]

Parents are good emotional coaches when they have high EQ themselves. Gottman identifies that emotionally intelligent parents:

- are aware of the emotions of the child,
- teach when emotional situations provide the opportunity ,
- listen and validate the feelings of the child without being critical or judgmental.

- teach the child to recognize and label emotions
- teach problem-solving while setting limits

Children will often express their own negative feelings in inappropriate ways, such as hitting or pushing. This can be a valuable learning opportunity for EQ if parents acknowledge the emotion behind the misbehavior, help the child label it, and then talk about how certain behaviors are inappropriate. The next step is helping the child to problem solve more appropriate ways of dealing with negative emotions. On the other hand, parents can actively destroy EQ by ignoring and being disrespectful of a child's feelings or by allowing any emotion as acceptable at any time.

> "There are very different emotional habits instilled by parents whose...infant's emotional needs are acknowledged and met or whose discipline includes empathy ...or self-absorbed parents who ignore a child's distress or who discipline capriciously by yelling and hitting."
>
> **–Daniel Goleman**

Little Donnie met his dad in the parenting room after class. Spying an empty pizza box in the trash, he demanded, "I want pizza now!" Donnie was hungry and got angry because there was no pizza for him. A temper tantrum was imminent. Dad prepared to sternly set some limits. Then he thought of a strategy he was learning in his parenting class and decided to change tactics:

- He acknowledged his son's emotions: "Man, I hate it when I'm hungry and there's no pizza left for me. Bummer!"

- He labeled the emotions for his son: "I bet you're angry that there isn't any pizza for you."

- He stated which behaviors were inappropriate: "Donnie, demanding pizza isn't going to help."

- He problem solved: "How's about we check the snack cupboard at home for something to tide you over until supper time."

> "Good parenting requires more than intellect....Good parenting involves emotion."
>
> **–John Gottman**

As parents, we want our children to experience a rich emotional life and have healthy relationships with others. With our coaching, children can become increasingly capable in EQ and reach their full potential. Because his father is an emotional coach for his son, someday Donnie, like Ibrahim, will attend his high school reunion having been successful in life.

TIME FOR ACTION!

For Parents to Do:

1. Using Success = IQ x EQ, estimate your success score by rating yourself on the IQ and EQ scales (1-10).

   A. What EQ skills do you wish to improve in yourself (see p. 34-35)?

   B. Identify situations or opportunities where you can improve your EQ skills.

2. Recall a past event of your child's misbehavior.

   A. What were your reactions and feelings during that event?

   B. What were your child's emotions during that event?

   C. What was the outcome of this event?

   D. How might your being aware of and acknowledging your child's emotions have changed the outcome?

3. Identify situations or opportunities where you can improve your child's EQ skills.

To Do with Your Child:

1. See Appendix C (p. 125), Books about Feelings, for children's books that give you opportunities to talk with your child about the emotions depicted in photos or illustrations and the cause and effect of behaviors on relationships.

2. Create opportunities for your child to practice waiting or delaying rewards until later, such as waiting at meal time for all family members to be served food before beginning to eat or helping with folding the laundry first before turning on the TV.

3. Look for ways to talk to your child about enthusiasm and a positive outlook when situations don't go as well as desired or planned.

4. Role play difficult situations that may occur when your child is playing with friends, such as fighting over toys, and talk about how these situations could be resolved.

5. Look for opportunities for coaching friendship skills such as greeting people, including others in groups or offering compliments.

CHAPTER 6

Star Qualities
Twinkle, Twinkle Little Star, How I Wonder WHO You Are.

"There must be more to life than having everything."
–Maurice Sendak

Ken and Molly settled in front of the TV to watch the red carpet arrivals of some of the biggest stars in show biz. Meanwhile, their parents read magazines about the latest criminal investigations of some of the very same stars.

"He has everything," said Ken, mesmerized by an actor's fame and wealth. "When I grow up, I want to be just like him. I'm going to be a star!" The parents looked up from their magazine, disturbed that their children saw this celebrity as someone to copy while they clearly saw that this famous person had an empty personal life.

Who doesn't want to be a star? Most people, at some point, have a fantasy about stardom. Money, talent, beauty and athleticism are all measures used to identify celebrities, but often societal measures of stardom and success are deceiving. Some of the brightest stars are never seen on TV or magazine covers. Just as stars in the sky give light and direction to others, so too with people who are true stars in life.

The children in the story are not looking at real and lasting success, but a shallow imitation. The stars that they should be admiring are those in real life who have the character qualities that fit the new formula for success: Success = EQ X IQ.

EQ TOOLS FOR SUCCESS

Various experts and authors have identified universal and longstanding characteristics that are tools for success. We call the tools for success in our own life story and that of our children **Star Qualities: the character and moral traits of a principled human being.** Star Qualities have the potential to transform and change our characters as adults and build hopeful futures for our child. They are not secret winning tactics that give our children a competitive edge over the neighbor kids during football tryouts or spelling bees. Rather, they are the underpinnings of a successful life and society. Some of these include being:

- **Courageous:** responding with meaningful action in spite of fear

- **Creative:** inventive, full of ideas; using ideas to solve problems

- **Curious:** desire to learn; willing to explore the unknown

- **Emotionally Aware:** able to recognize and deal with feelings and thoughts of self and others

- **Focused:** staying fixed on a goal or task; filtering out distractions to stay fixed on what's important

- **Optimistic:** hopeful, seeing the positive perspective

- **Organized:** able to keep one's life in order so that problems and conflicts are limited

- **Outgoing:** friendly, sociable; able to relate well with others

- **Persistent:** persevere, follow through until a task is completed

- **Proactive:** analyzing and anticipating problems; doing what needs to be done before a problem develops

- **Responsible:** accountable, reliable and dependable

- **Self-Confident:** belief in oneself; an "I can do it" attitude

- **Self-Disciplined:** in control of emotions and actions; delay gratification

- **Self-Motivated:** self-starting; doing what needs to be done without waiting for others to lead

- **Spiritual:** connected with one's true principles and values; seeking beyond self for meaning to life

The Star Qualities Appendix (p. 114) features activities that will enhance your understanding of these qualities and help you develop specific Star Qualities in your children.

ROADBLOCKS TO SUCCESS

Just as Star Qualities enhance potential, negative mental habits are roadblocks to success:

- **Anger:** being annoyed
- **Judgmental:** being critical
- **Self-Doubt:** being unsure of self
- **Sarcasm:** mean-spirited remarks
- **Jealousy:** envy
- **Procrastination:** putting things off
- **Self-centered:** inconsiderate of others

- **Boredom:** having no interest
- **Worry:** being anxious, nervous or troubled
- **Pessimism:** anticipating negative results
- **Meanness:** malicious, unkind
- **Apathy:** loss of will to care
- **Grudges:** hanging on to ill will toward others

Just as we work to build Star Qualities, we need to work to eliminate negative mental habits that keep us from our full potential.

DEVELOPMENTAL NEWS FLASH!!!

Common to family life are children's misbehaviors and parents' unrealistic expectations. Awareness of child development will help us understand our children's behaviors and have realistic expectations while we patiently promote the development of Star Qualities.

• **The moral development of young children is not yet mature.** Star Qualities and building character are connected to moral development. All of these blossom slowly over time. Dr. Thomas Lickona, in *Raising Good Children,* states, "Kids are not short adults. Parents are often surprised to learn that kids' moral reasoning is so different from their own."[5] A moral foundation is laid in the early years by parents who understand development and have appropriate expectations.

• **Young children are concrete learners.** They are limited in their ability to picture and talk about invisible qualities like responsibility or courage. Therefore, they are able to apply what they are learning about such concepts only occasionally and often with difficulty. We can prepare them for success by being realistic about what our children are capable of and what skills they still need time to master.

STAR QUALITIES REQUIRE POLISH

If we want our children to have Star Qualities as adults, we must put in **intentional effort** as parents now. If children are left to pick up Star Qualities by chance, we may be disappointed. Life may teach them the negative mental habits instead.

> Lucy watched in amazement as the children of her friend, Shaquilla, cleared off the dinner table. The eldest child carried the dishes away and the youngest asked if she could sweep under the table. Lucy wished her own children would be as responsible. "The kids always have jobs to do after dinner," Shaquilla explained to Lucy. "It was the same when I was a kid and I want my children to learn the same skills."

"One shining quality lends luster to another, or hides some glaring defect."

–William Hazlitt

Each child's unique temperament influences the starting point of devleopment for some Star Qualities (outgoing, persistent, self-discipline, focused and optimstic), therefore providing natural advantages or difficulties in their growth. Because all human beings have relative strengths and weaknesses, all Star Qualities need to be honed and polished in order for people to reach their full potential. Robert Sternberg says successful people "know their strengths; they know their weaknesses. They capitalize on their strengths; they compensate for or correct their weaknesses."[6]

TIME FOR ACTION!

For Parents to Do:

1. What Star Qualities (p. 41) shine in you? Which need some polishing? What negative mental habits (p. 42) can get in your way?

2. Learn more about how to develop Star Qualities in adults and children in Appendix A (p. 114).

To Do with Your Child:

1. What shining Star Qualities are already emerging in your child?

2. Have you in any way discouraged the growth of Star Qualities in your child?

3. What Star Qualities do you wish to strengthen? Find specific activities for developing these qualities in Appendix A (p. 114).

CHAPTER 7

Observation
Discovering Your Child

"One should not make sweeping statements about children (or a particular child)....one should only make statements based on observations of reality!"

–Magda Gerber

"To help us get in touch with using observation as a parenting tool, your assignment is to walk around this building for fifteen minutes and write down anything that you observe. There are no suggestions about what you should be observing, so write down anything you notice." When introducing the skill of observation to parenting classes, Elaine often starts out with this activity. As the parents share, it is obvious that while observing the same building, each has experienced it differently. Some noticed sounds, others observed colors and light, yet others focused on various textures. This task often brings out anxiety in parents since they are inexperienced in observation and wonder if they saw the right things.

Observation means to pay attention, watch, perceive or notice. It is a critical tool in our Top 20 Parenting toolbox that helps us collect more information to get to know our children better. It helps us use the Frame with more clarity and take in more details as we analyze the Big Picture of our children's behaviors. Observation 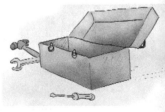 builds EQ, Star Qualities and awareness of Above or Below the Line. It is a respectful way to spend time with our children to learn more about them as unique people with strengths, weaknesses, preferences and patterns. [7]

PRACTICING OBSERVATION

Parents are busy people without large blocks of time to sit around observing. However, using any small snippet of time to intentionally observe can add up to knowing a child better.

It takes practice to put ourselves in a child's place well enough to understand why and how behavior happens. Knowing where our children are developmentally helps us focus on a particular task or behavior and imagine ourselves in their places.

Like the parents in Elaine's class, we may wonder if we are observing the correct things. Everything observed helps us know our children better. In all areas of life, being a good observer leads to understanding and respect of others. The more that we are aware, the deeper we drink in the richness of family life.

Parents can become more skilled at observation by practicing the following:

• watching without judging good or bad, right or wrong,

• focusing on the child, while putting aside our own agenda and thoughts,

• concentrating on a particular task or behavior the child is doing,

• listening and watching quietly without taking over,

• sensing what the child is feeling.

DEVELOPMENTAL NEWS FLASH

• **Everything children do is done with a purpose.** Without the benefit of years of experience, young children try to solve problems through trial and error. What appears to have no logical reason to adults can be a deeply meaningful action to children.

• **From their point of view, everything children do is 'right' at the time they are doing it.** Children have a different point of view and different motives for behavior than adults. Their intention is not to misbehave or to be manipulative. They are simply trying to discover what works.

OBSERVATION IS HARD TO DO

Observation can be difficult because as parents we play three similtaneous roles.

•We are parents of our children.

•We are still children of our parents.

•We are adults with our own interests and needs.

Because of these roles, we may be looking at our children through various lenses that give us conflicting feelings about what we see.

Consider the thoughts of a father observing his child playing with a pail of soapy water in the back yard.

Being aware of this conflict and what we are seeing about the child and our self will help us determine the best balance between these roles.

WHEN SHOULD PARENTS INTERVENE?

Sometimes what we observe may seem like misbehavior when it might more accurately be called **childish** behavior. For instance, children are naturally curious. Curiosity could lead little Susan to pull off the shiny green leaves from potted plants. From her point of view, what she is doing is only natural for a child. A parent might think her actions are wrong.

While observing our children, we might notice something that requires intervention. How do we know whether or not we should intervene? Always intervene in matters of safety. A parent can intervene in ways that respect a child's point of view and purpose, then redirect the behavior and watch how the situation plays out. For example, Tyrell was hitting the glass window with his toy hammer. His father quickly grabbed the hammer and said, "I see you want to pound. Windows break. Let's find something you can pound." After pointing to the toy workbench, Tyrell's father watched as his son hammered the colorful wooden pegs.

TIME FOR ACTION!

For Parents to Try:

1. Go on an observation walk with a friend in your neighborhood, at a mall or at a park. Write down anything you see. Compare lists. Notice differences and similarities. Let the differences lead to a broader understanding of observation and point of view.

2. Observe your child at play. Write down anything you notice. What did you learn about him? Do your observations have a common theme? What did you learn about yourself? Narrow your scope in observing your child. Look for something specific each day, like cute sayings, mannerisms, vocabulary words, habits or play patterns.

To Try with Your Child:

1. Go on an Observation Walk with your child focusing on the five senses. What did you learn about your child's observation style?

2. Take another Observation Walk to find, count or collect items from a specific category, such as rocks, bugs, flowers, leaves or cars.

CHAPTER 8

Goals
Dreams with Deadlines

"There are few successful adults who were not at first successful children."
–Alexander Chase

"I hate when goals come up in class," one parent whispered to another in the parenting class. "I never know what to write as family goals. I just want the kids to behave."

"Me, too. I don't have time for goals. I just hope my son turns out ok as an adult."

"Making it through the day is my only goal," said a third parent. "I let the kids watch more TV than I want just so I can survive. I can't bear to think what all the TV viewing will do to my kids down the line."

Many people have never made goal setting part of their life. They coast from event to event without directing their lives toward a specific destination. However, another Top 20 Parenting tool for unlocking potential is establishing and working towards goals.

GOALS ARE DREAMS WITH DEADLINES

Goals are a powerful strategy for bettering our best. They direct and give focus to our lives. Goals alert us when we get off course and help us get back on track. They make sure that our effort and time are not wasted. They ask us not to settle for "I hope it all works out," but to reach out for what we want in life. Like a map for a traveler, they guide us to where we want to be.

Top 20 Parents know that without having goals and determining means for achieving them their dreams drift aimlessly without ever being attained. For example, a parent might say, "I'd like my child to be a reader," but the parent may not carve out time to read with the child.

SETTING SMART GOALS

Goals can be long term, spanning years ("I want my child to finish high school") or short term, spanning just a few hours or days ("I want my child to nap this afternoon"). Goals can be parent-oriented ("I want to get time today to take a hot bath") or child-oriented ("I want my child to have fun at the park"). But goals should always be **SMART**.

In order to be effective and achievable, goals need to include five important characteristics: specific, measurable, action oriented, realistic and time limited.

Specific: To be effective, goals need to be specific. Wanting to be a better parent or wanting a child to be a better reader are too vague to be helpful. Having a specific goal keeps our attention and energy focused so we can direct our efforts.

Vague: To be a better parent
Specific: To understand 3–year–old language development

Measurable: Measurable goals provide a way of getting feedback so we know if we are progressing towards our goals. For instance, if a goal is to read five books to her child by the end of the week, a parent can keep score. If she reads one book on Tuesday and two books on Thursday, she can evaluate and read two more books by Friday.

Action Oriented: A SMART goal also focuses on the action needed to achieve the desired results. Action oriented goals focus our attention and energy.

Non–action Oriented: To be a better parent
Action Oriented: Read a library book on child development; enroll in an eight-week parenting class

Realistic: Goals are intended to stretch and challenge us and yet be within our reach. Whereas unattainable goals frustrate us, realistic goals motivate us. It would be wonderful if we could be a perfect parent but that is not a realistic goal. Striving for an unrealistic goal can get us lost just as surely as having no goal at all.

We also need to be realistic about the time it takes to reach our goals. It's unrealistic to expect that we would know all there is about language development by quickly reading a pamphlet in a doctor's office.

Time Limited: Setting a deadline for achieving our goals helps to avoid procrastination and motivates us toward our goals. If we merely wish for things to happen, they probably never will.

Not Time Limited: I will expose my child to literacy.
Time Limited: I will get my child to Library Story Time once
this week.

SMART GOAL = SPECIFIC + MEASURABLE + ACTION ORIENTED
+ REALISTIC + TIME LIMITED

DEVELOPMENTAL NEWS FLASH!!!

Young children develop according to biological design and individual unfolding. Adult goals for children need to acknowledge that children are works in progress. What should be stressed in goals for our children is improvement and not perfection.

*"Progress, not perfection
is the goal."*

–Mary Sheedy Kurcinka

BARRIERS TO ACHIEVING GOALS

Just as physical barriers on a road keep us from reaching our destination, three mental barriers can get in the way of goals.

1. **Rationalizing:** convincing ourselves that something isn't very important. This can occur before setting a goal or after failing to achieve one.

    Example: I wanted to join a parenting group, but it probably won't be worth my time.

2. **Justifying:** defending the excuses we make that keep us from our goals.

   Example: I wanted to join a parenting class, but it was on Saturdays and sometimes my friend visits on Saturdays.

3. **Procrastinating:** putting off acting in our Best Interest.

   Example: Someday when I have more time I'm going to take a parenting class, but not now.

> "It is a most mortifying reflection for a man to consider what he has done, compared to what he might have done."
>
> —Samuel Johnson

PARENTING FEARS

A major roadblock to achieving our goals is fear. Fear prevents us from moving forward and erodes our potential for achieving our dreams. Fear can keep our goals from taking flight.

In our roles as parents, fear can show in several ways.

Fear of Failure: Many of us fear not being a good enough parent. Children don't come with operating manuals. Even when parents have read lots of child rearing books, they may feel they cannot apply the information to the real child in their home when issues arise.

Top 20 Parents learn to see failure as a detour sign guiding them to find the right route in achieving goals. They know they can learn something in the experience of failure that helps them discover the way to ultimate success.

> "If you expect to have perfect children you will be constantly disappointed and your children constantly frustrated. If you realize that your children are perfectly themselves in every moment, you and your children will be at peace."
>
> —Lao Tzu Tao Te Ching
> Adapted by William Martin

Fear of Rejection: The fear of rejection revolves around the relationship between parent and child. Often children communicate with temper tantrums or shouting, "I hate you." What a young child means is "I don't like what you are making me do or what you are keeping me from doing right now. I will like you again later." A family is a complex web of emotions and members may not like each other now and again. However, love is more enduring than the daily misunderstandings and rejections that are part of family life.

Fear of Humiliation and Embarrassment: What parent hasn't been humiliated by the behavior of a child in public. The behavior of our children is linked to our own self-esteem as parents. The loss of self-esteem through embarrassment can immobilize parents from achieving their goals.

Fear of Other People's Opinions: The fear of other people's opinions is constantly looming because we are always receiving other people's messages about ourselves and our children. Other people's opinions can cause us to question ourselves and jab at our self-esteem, our methods and our goals. As will be covered in more depth in chapter twelve, we must often decide when to accept or disregard other peoples' opinions.

REACHING GOALS: BEING COMMITTED AND WISE

Every goal worth striving for has some degree of struggle or adversity attached to it. Our ability to achieve a goal has a lot to do with our commitment. No goal gets accomplished without commitment.

Commitment can be compared to climbing a mountain.

Climbers: high commitment— "I'm in no matter what."

Campers: some commitment— "I'm in as long as it's easy."

Quiters: no commitment— "I'm out."

Top 20 thinkers use the **WISE** method to build their persistence and assure that they achieve their goals:

Willpower: Not succumbing to temptations; having self-discipline.

Initiative: Self-starting, using the power that comes from within us.

Stamina: The strength to continue when we're tired or don't feel like it.

Enthusiasm: Having the passion to achieve the goal; finding pleasure and enjoyment in the process.

Despite fears and barriers that might get in the way, goal setting is a powerful part of Top 20 Parenting. We need to keep our dreams for ourselves and our children alive and bring them to fruition by keeping them in mind during our day to–day decision making.

For Parents to Do:

1. Think about a past completed personal goal, such as losing weight or starting a new hobby. What was your willpower, initiative, stamina and enthusiasm level when chasing after your dream? What helped you achieve this goal? What barriers did you experience?

2. Write down a SMART goal for yourself now. Make sure it's specific, measurable, action oriented, realistic and time limited. Identify your commitment level for the goal. Develop an action plan for this goal and check in after one week.

To Do with Your Child:

1. Talk to your child about her short term plans for the day. What is something she would like to accomplish? How can you help her accomplish this goal?

2. Talk with your child about the future. What does he want to be when he grows up? How can you develop his fascination and knowledge about a special topic?

3. Help your child make lists of tasks, chores or activities to be done. Guide her to use the list to accomplish what the list describes.

CHAPTER 9

Temperament
Why Are They Acting Like That?

"The errors hardest to condone in other people are one's own."

–Piet Hein

Life was filled with fireworks at the Ortega house. Maria couldn't understand why she and her young son, Brian, would clash over simple things like putting on shoes or throwing away broken toys. There seemed to be no relief in sight until Maria learned about the nine temperament traits and what a big piece of the puzzle temperament was in dealing with her son. She and Brian shared many of the same traits. Maria realized that they often clashed because she hated seeing her own traits in him.

Many parents want to improve their children's behavior. In order to make changes, Top 20 Parents understand the uniqueness of their kids and that behavior is influenced by temperament. They realize that temperament is one of the essential puzzle pieces to understanding each child.

Temperament refers to untrained reactions and behavior style. The term comes from the Latin verb 'temperore' meaning 'to mix'. Temperament is a unique mix, a combination of behaviors. Temperament traits chart human reactions to events, changes and environments. **A child's temperament is the package of social, emotional and physiological factors that nature bestows on each human.** This bundle includes strengths, weaknesses and lots of potential. But temperament is not destiny. We can adjust, augment or heighten what nature gives us.

"There is much to be gained by appreciating differences, and much to be lost by ignoring them or condemning them."

–D. Kiersey

TEMPERAMENT TRAITS

Temperament styles are not right or wrong. They're merely the collection of personality cards we are dealt. We do not have to play them all and can work to create new strengths to our hand as personality develops. What's important is to know what the temperament traits are and be able to recognize what they look like in both ourselves and our children.

Pioneers in the field of temperament research, including Stella Chess and Alexander Thomas, have identified nine temperament traits.[8]

TEMPERAMENT TRAITS

Activity: the daily proportion of active periods (moving, running, fidgeting) and quiet periods (resting, relaxing, playing quietly). An active child may be noisy and constantly engaged in action.

Regularity: the predictability or unpredictability of biological functions (hunger, sleeping and bowel elimination) affecting a person's ability to cope with schedules and routines. An irregular child may be difficult for a parent seeking to establish a family routine.

Approach vs Withdrawal: the first reaction to a new situation, person or thing. Approachability is seen in a child whose first reactions may include smiling, engagement and interest in a new experience. Withdrawal reactions are crying, moving away, refusal to try, tantrums or stomach aches.

Adaptability: the ease to which a person is able to adapt to change in schedules, routines or situations. A child with low adaptability expresses long-term levels of stress, disappointment, confusion, uncooperativeness or anger.

Sensory Threshold: the intensity of reaction to how things taste, feel, smell, look and sound. A sensitive child reacts to bright lights, loud music, the emotions of others, temperature, colors, tags in clothing and food textures leading quickly to over stimulation.

Quality of Mood: the balance of time spent happy, smiling, optimistic, content and social compared to the time spent serious, analytical, withdrawn, sad or cranky. A child with a predominantly negative mood may be whiny, critical, tearful and seem ungrateful.

Intensity of Reactions. the strength of a positive or negative emotional reaction to events, people or things. An intense child's powerful reactions are characterized by loud laughter and happy outbursts or screams, tears and tantrums. Low intensity is characterized by calm, quiet and mild reactions.

Distractibility: the degree to which a person is distracted by people, colors, noises and objects in the environment. Because a highly distractible child cannot filter outside stimuli, he loses focus on tasks or parental requests.

Persistence: the continuation of an activity in the face of obstacles and difficulties. A persistent child is focused on completing an activity without quitting. She can stay determined for a long time, regardless of a lack of success or rewards.

TEMPERAMENT CLUSTERS

Although temperament traits can be understood individually, they often cluster in predictable ways. Chess and Thomas identified three temperament patterns that can influence interactions between parents and children: the easy child, the slow-to-warm-up child and the difficult child.[9]

Easy Child: Is regular in biological function, approaches new situations positively, is adaptable to change, and has a positive mood.

Slow-to-warm-up Child: Responds negatively to new situations and adapts slowly, while reacting mildly to events.

Difficult Child: Has irregular biological functions, has negative withdrawal reactions to new people and situations, is slow to adapt to change and exhibits intense and negative moods. This grouping is labeled 'difficult' because parents typically have difficulties managing their behavior.

DEVELOPMENTAL NEWS FLASH!!!

• **Development plays a role in the behavior of young children.** The development of children can confuse our understanding of temperament if we are not looking at the Big Picture. For instance, all toddlers are somewhat active and persistent. Only observation over time will tell whether a child is more active or persistent than the norm. It is useful to observe our children with temperament in mind so we will better understand their individuality, keeping in mind that their behaviors may change as they mature.

WHAT TEMPERAMENT MEANS FOR PARENTING

Many parents get frustrated with the 'hand' their child is dealt. For example, if a parent hopes to have a socially outgoing child, the parent may get impatient with a child that is slow-to-warm up. Top 20 Parents develop an awareness of their children's temperaments when creating appropriate expectations and goals for their children.

In families, people with a variety of temperaments live together. A match or mismatch in personality affects family relationships. Any family member's temperament can change the environment of a family. Imagine the clashes that might result when a low activity parent and a high activity child wait in a crowded doctor's office. While temperament traits are not right or wrong, certain traits can be perceived by parents, relatives or teachers as irritations or weaknesses.

Sometimes a family environment can be negatively affected when parent and child share the same temperament traits as in the opening story. Maria and her son fought because she unwittingly reacted negatively to seeing the same temperament traits in Brian as in herself. Parents can both enjoy or be irritated by similarities and differences they have with their children.

Knowledge of temperament as a puzzle piece and how it affects behaviors and interactions between family members allows the parenting journey to be more pleasant. Top 20 Parents know that all personalities can and must be molded for our best potential. Appendix B can be used by parents to better understand their own and their child's temperaments and to gain insight on how temperament affects behavior and human interactions.

> "When I figured out who Andy is, it helped me to see many of the things he does. He does these things because of temperament. Now a lot of things make sense."
>
> –A Mom

For Parents to Do:

1. Assess your own temperament by using the Temperament Rating Scale (Appendix B, p. 122). Which traits have been a challenge for you or for others? What is the positive aspect of that challenging trait?

2. Identify temperament traits of all the members of your family. How do these traits affect your family relationships and environment?

3. To better understand temperament and its connection to child behaviors, read other experts in the field, such as Mary Sheedy Kurcinka's *Raising Your Spirited Child* and Stanley Greenspan's *The Challenging Child*.

To Do with Your Child:

1. Assess your child's temperament by using the Temperament Rating Scale (Appendix B, 122). Consider one of your child's temperament traits that is a challenge for you. What is a positive aspect of this trait for your child?

2. Help your child become aware of her own temperament traits by narrating situations as they happen or replaying a situation with her. For instance, "I know you really want to finish this puzzle. You're very persistent. Because we have to leave Susie's house soon, what would you like to finish before we leave?"

3. Look for times to observe your child's temperament style, like unexpected schedule changes, surprise visits or new situations. How does your child's temperament style affect his behavior in these situations?

CHAPTER 10

Responding to Hits
Life Happens. What Are We Going to Do about It?

"Although the world is full of suffering, it is full also of the overcoming of it."
–Helen Keller

"I guess it's just my turn," sighed Shirley as she told her husband the list of Hits that happened that day. "The water heater went out while doing laundry. I called our regular plumber but she's on vacation. Then school called. Zach had thrown up twice and I needed to get him right away. I finally got a plumber who just left. That's why we're eating last night's leftovers for supper. And I never got my work article written before my deadline."

Then Shirley chuckled, "Zach's excited to skip his bedtime bath. And you know what, I'm ok with that too. The best thing for me is to take a walk after the kids go to bed."

Shirley illustrates a Top 20 response to **hits, the unexpected negative events** we encounter along the road of life that can knock us off course. They're invitations to go Below the Line. When Hits occur, we can either react impulsively or respond thoughtfully. In either case, how we handle Hits will affect our journey in life.

Examples of typical Hits for parents include:

• Bad events at work that hang over our heads at home,

• Getting a phone call about our children's negative behavior,

• Missing an anticipated event because we have a sick child,

• Being dumped by non-parenting friends because we have children,

• Receiving hurtful comments about our parenting decisions or post-pregnancy appearance,

• Mechanical problems with the car, computer or appliances.

Examples of typical Hits for children include:

- Being told 'No' when wanting to do something.

- Insults or teasing about appearance or lack of ability.

- Breaking a favorite toy.

- Being rejected by a playmate.

- Missing an anticipated event because of sickness.

HANDLING HITS

Top 20 and Bottom 80 thinkers deal with Hits differently. When Bottom 80s receive Hits, they immediately react based on their feelings. They are emotionally impulsive. The first action of Top 20s is to pause, knowing that a Hit invites us to immediately drop Below the Line. During this brief pause, Top 20s determine a useful response that's in their Best Interest. Therefore, a Top 20 response tends to move towards a solution to a problem while a Bottom 80 reaction, like shouting at a store clerk, creates a second problem worse than the first.

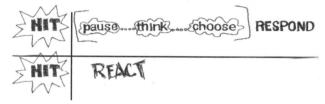

"In adversity remember to keep an even mind."

–Horace

The following diagram illustrates the difference between Top 20 and Bottom 80 thinking.

FEELINGS FROM HITS	BOTTOM 80 REACTIONS TO HITS	
• Angry	• Being defensive	• Seeking revenge
• Depressed	• Withdrawing	• Swearing
• Embarrassed	• Being apathetic	• Fighting verbally
• Worried	• Attacking	or physically
• Humiliated	• Being sarcastic	• Crying
• Hurt	• Sulking	• Backbiting
• Unappreciated		
• Powerless	**TOP 20 RESPONSES TO HITS**	
• Overwhelmed	• Pause and assess the situation	• Seek information from others
• Stupid	• Act to solve problem	• Seek support from friends
• Defeated	• Acknowledge limitations	• Prevent the same Hit from happening again
• Frustrated	• Realize that sometimes it's 'My Turn' for things to happen	• Maintain dignity while Below the Line by protecting yourself and others from harm
• Afraid	• Use a Trampoline to get Above the Line	
• Confused		

PERSPECTIVE

In families, adults and children may have different perspectives about whether or not something is a Hit. For example, a four-year-old child might come bounding down the steps carrying a special picture she has drawn for grampa. Tearing the picture in her exuberance, she may be sorrowfully disappointed. Oblivious that the torn picture constitutes a Hit to his daughter, a dad might say, "Sweetie, you can just make another picture later." He unknowingly makes the situation worse by sending his daughter running out of the room in howls of despair.

Conversely, children may not recognize Hits that parents experience because they have little understanding of a grown up's world. If a parent loses a job, a child may not recognize the stress of a parent and react inappropriately to the news, making matters worse.

RESPONSE-ABILITY

Hits hurt. A common reaction to a Hit is to hit back and that's seldom in anyone's Best Interest. Top 20s have developed the habit of **response-ability** which is **the ability to choose a response to a Hit that is in the Best Interest of all concerned.**

Response-ability has two dimensions: **Stability and Resiliency.**

Stability is the ability to take a Hit. Top 20s are better able to take a Hit without reacting in a negative way. Bottom 80s tend to rank low in stability and pay a price for that.

Mr. Cody returned a test to his student, Antonio. The test was graded "F." Seeing the poor grade, Antonio yelled a swear word. After scolding Antonio, Mr. Cody offered him a second chance. The student crumpled the exam and tossed it over the teacher's shoulder. Antonio was then escorted to the Dean's office where he was able to think about three failures: one math test + two stability tests.

Resiliency is the ability to bounce back after taking a Hit. Highly resilient people are able to get beyond the Hit and move on. People with low resilience relive the Hit over and over. Shirley showed resiliency by being good-humored and laughing at her situation by the end of the day. She knew that a walk would help her feel ready to face the next day's challenges. If she wasn't resilient, Shirley would grumble about that day into the next week, making her son feel guilty for getting stomach flu. The focus needed to catch up on the work assignment would be hampered by her own brooding and negativity. A common low resiliency response of a Bottom 80 is to hold a grudge.

"The growth of wisdom may be gauged exactly by the diminution of ill-temper."

–Nietzsche

DEVELOPMENTAL NEWS FLASH

• **Young children do not accurately see the connection of cause and effect in situations.** Explaining that Hits are not caused by something the child did may need to be repeated over and over.

• **Self-concept in young children is immature.** Still developing their self-concept, what they believe about themselves, children are vulnerable to how Hits affect them. Their stability and resiliency may be on very shaky ground. However, the early childhood years are an ideal time to strengthen self–concept, stability and resiliency by using Hits to teach appropriate responses. Role playing is a fun learning strategy to build confidence in handling life's challenges. A parent and child can reenact a past Hit and act out alternate responses for 'Next Time'. While role playing, a parent can introduce and practice the strategy of Pause-Think-Choose with a child.

Sometimes the Hits children receive come from their own parents. For example, "We didn't want another child, let alone a brat like you who can't keep her room clean. You're a pig!" If parents are reacting to their own Hits by lashing out when they are Below the Line, then they are less likely to respond in the Best Interest of their child's growing self-concept.

'MY TURN'

Life happens. Hits are part of life and can't be completely avoided. A Top 20 way of looking at Hits is simply realizing that sometimes it will just be 'my turn' for irritating things to happen. Once in awhile

• the shopping cart in the parking lot scratches my car,

• bird poop lands on my head,

• the passing car splashes the puddle on my new coat,

• a child has a temper tantrum at a restaurant,

• we need to clean a big diaper mess just before an important appointment.

Top 20 Parents realize that since it will eventually be their turn for Hits, they need to be prepared and practice the Response process:

> **Pause-> Think-> Choose.**

Knowing that our children are not immune to Hits because it's sometimes 'their turn', we can also prepare them for these scenarios.

For Parents to Do:

1. Recall a time when your reaction to a Hit made the situation worse. Replay past Hits and think of how you can improve your response 'Next Time'.

2. Consider Hits you tend to react to and those to which you thoughtfully respond. Visualize a more thoughtful response to the Hits to which you typically react.

3. On a scale of 1-5, rate your stability and resiliency when taking a Hit. How can you improve your stability and resiliency?

To Do with Your Child:

1. Discuss Hits your child may experience in the near future and role play how he could respond. For example, "What will you do if a child does not want to share a toy with you even if you ask politely?"

2. Talk about causes and effects, explaining when an event is NOT your child's fault. For instance, "The car didn't break down because we drove back to Billie's house to get your doll."

3. How can you help your child improve stability and resiliency?

4. Explain and practice with your child the Pause-Think-Choose strategy in formulating responses to Hits. Point out when reactions are not in her Best Interest.

CHAPTER 11

Building the Trust Fund
The Key to Respectful Relationships

"Without feelings of respect, what is there to distinguish men from Beasts?"
–Confucius

It was hard for Thao to trust his son's story since little Bao had been caught lying about a toy hidden in his pocket last week. Today Bao reassured his father that the whistle that he just brought home from preschool had been a gift from his teacher. Thao paused for a moment before responding to his son. Over the past week, Bao had lied about eating all the cookies, failed to put away his bike and disrespected his grandmother when she came to take care of the children. Thao knew that his relationship with his son would be affected by the actions he would take. He decided that forgiving Bao and giving him another chance to be trusted would let the boy see that he was loved and respected.

One of the most important things to human beings is relationships. Everyone needs and desires close and meaningful connections with others. These important relationships and connections are strengthened by trust and respect.

Trust is the firm belief in the honesty and reliability of another person. It is an essential nutrient that a young child needs to develop. As newborns, babies must trust the world for survival. They will not thrive physically or emotionally if they do not sense that they can trust their caregivers to consistently and adequately meet their needs. For toddlers to grow they must feel enough confidence about the world to test their independence by disagreeing with their caregivers and physically moving away from the safety of a trusted adult.

THE TRUST FUND

Think of a checking account at the bank. Money is put in and taken out. For finances to work smoothly, more money needs to go in than gets taken out. In his book *The Seven Habits of Highly Effective People,* Stephen Covey uses this bank account metaphor to explain how trust is built or lost in a relationship.[10]

The strength of our Trust Fund is determined by deposits and withdrawals. We make **deposits** when we add to or grow our trust with others. We take **withdrawals** when we reduce or weaken our trust with others. Examples of these include:

Deposits	Withdrawals
Being nice: kind, courteous	Being mean: unkind, discourteous
Telling the truth	Lying
Keeping promises	Breaking promises
Speaking well of those who are absent	Dishonoring the absent
Being responsible	Blaming or making excuses
Apologizing	Needing to be right
Forgiving	Holding a grudge
Respecting the differences and needs of others	Disrespecting differences or needs of others

THE TRUST FUND AND TOP 20 PARENTING

The Trust Fund metaphor describes how we feel when we are treated well (deposits) and treated poorly (withdrawals). It is hard to resolve conflict and keep connected in a relationship with a Trust Fund deficit. Life is more pleasant and productive if we can create a more positive balance.

"To avoid being overdrawn, balance your accounts daily. With each day our lives change...Take a moment at the end of each day to review your deposits and withdrawals."

–Greg Henry Quinn

A positive balance allows for understanding and forgiveness when family members make mistakes or take withdrawals. It is reassuring to know that the account is strong enough to withstand the human imperfections that go along with daily living.

Awareness of the Trust Fund is a Top 20 Parenting tool that can strengthen trust and respect in families and restore balance to relationships that have too many withdrawals. A high positive Trust Fund in the family is necessary for children to grow and reach their potential.

> "Every child has an emotional tank, a place of emotional strength that can fuel him through the challenging days of childhood and adolescence. Just as cars are powered by reserves in the gas tank, our children are fueled from their emotional tanks. We must fill our children's emotional tanks for them to operate as they should and reach their potential."
>
> **Gary Chapman and Ross Campbell**

THE IMPACT OF CHILD DEVELOPMENT ON THE TRUST FUND

By not understanding the developmental stages, a parent can misinterpret a child's actions and intentions. The child's imperfect efforts may look like withdrawals to the parent, even if the child is trying to please and make a deposit to the Trust Fund.

- A parent having an unrealistic standard of neatness may overreact to an uncoordinated preschooler spilling milk.

- A parent may interpret a child's forgetfulness to say 'please' or 'thank you' as being intentionally rude.

We can be impatient as parents in wanting our deposits to grow quickly into a vast resource. Although we can be disappointed when a child's progress appears to be slow, development is happening in a natural progression. Reminding us of the growth of a bamboo tree, Stephen Covey encourages patience and perseverence. After nurturing a tree for four years, no growth is evident. However, in the fifth year the tree grows 80 feet, a growth that occurs because of the strong roots system underground. The beauty of the bamboo tree is worth the wait. Similarly, just as our deposits and trust will bear fruit in our children's lives years from now.

DEVELOPMENTAL NEWS FLASH!!!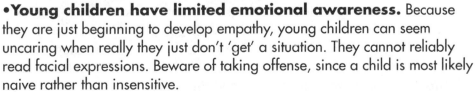

•**Young children have limited emotional awareness.** Because they are just beginning to develop empathy, young children can seem uncaring when really they just don't 'get' a situation. They cannot reliably read facial expressions. Beware of taking offense, since a child is most likely naive rather than insensitive.

•**Young children are egocentric.** The behaviors of young children revolve around their self-centered wants. A lot of child behavior that adults see as misbehaving is actually development doing what it is supposed to do. For example,

- they are curious and get into things they shouldn't.

- they have emotional meltdowns in stores because they impulsively want something or are tired.

Their egocentric 'misbehavior' is not directed at the parent as a withdrawal.

•**The memory skills of young children are immature.** They do not always have a firm grasp of the truth and may not remember past experiences accurately. Although children may appear to 'lie', these are likely to be inventive tales and should not be interpreted as intentionally malicious withdrawals.

•**Young children are concrete learners.** They do not grasp abstract concepts, like trust, as easily as concrete concepts. Even if children understood trust in one situation, they may not in another situation.

•**The cause and effect of emotional situations and relationships is not well understood.** Initially, children may unwittingly make withdrawals or deposits in our Trust Fund without understanding the consequences of their actions.

THE LAW OF BIG THINGS

Big Things are those things that are most important to us. From a very early age, the Big Thing for children is **Space.** Toddlers run from us on the playground because their bodies need more physical space and they need to be away from the adults that are their emotional home base. They need Space to grow up and experience life beyond their own backyards. This desire comes from deep inside. They're wired for this. It's natural and necessary. Of course, they keep us in sight while they climb on the playgrond equipment and run back to us when they skin a knee. However, once they feel secure and safe and that we are within reach, they're off again.

The Big Thing for parents is **Peace of Mind.** As parents, we have Peace of Mind when we know our kids are safe. When our children are young, we can secure Peace of Mind by controlling what they do, where they go and with whom they play. When lacking Peace of Mind, parents feel the urge to clamp down on a growing child's need for Space.

If children and parents help each other get the Big Things, their relationship will be smoother and more satisfying. If either doesn't get these Big Things, the relationship will be rocky and unsatisfying.

UNCONDITIONAL LOVE

The Trust Fund is about understanding trust and respect; it is not about earning or quantifying love. In adult relationships, we would expect both people to be contributing somewhat equally to the Trust Fund. If there is a significant imbalance, a friendship may end.

However, families are different. Parents cannot expect a young child to contribute equally to the Trust Fund. The adult in a parent/child relationship needs to take much more responsibility for contributing to the Trust Fund. A child's natural immaturity prevents him from contributing equally to the Trust Fund. We must give our children much more than they give us. This inequality requires from parents unconditional love, which does not expect or demand a settling of accounts.

> "If I love them only when they meet my... expectations, they will feel incompetent and will believe it is pointless to do their best, since it is never enough. They will always be plagued by insecurity, anxiety, low self-esteem, and anger. To guard against this, I need to often remind myself of my responsibility for their total growth... If I love them unconditionally, they will feel comfortable about themselves..."
>
> –Gary Chapman and Ross Campbell

For Parents to Do:

1. Reflect on actions or words of people in your past that affected your trust in them. What increased your trust? What weakened your trust?

2. Consider a relationship where your Trust Fund is low. What specific deposits could you make to increase the trust and respect in this account?

3. Think about deposits that you value in your family. Are there misunderstandings that occur because family members value or interpret certain deposits or withdrawals differently?

To Do with Your Child:

1. What does your child consider a deposit? A withdrawal? How does your child like to give and receive love?

2. Observe for indicators that your child is developing trust in caregivers, relatives and play situations.

3. Which of your child's behaviors are showing you her need for Space? How can you have Peace of Mind while providing her Space?

4. Point out to your child the effects of his positive and negative behavior so that awareness of the Trust Fund can develop.

CHAPTER 12

The Influence of Messages
Fact or Fiction

"Man's most valuable trait is a judicious sense of what not to believe."

–Euripides

"Your face is blue!" an intimidating girl told kindergartner Sharon on the playground. Sharon immediately ran all the way home to ask her mother, Helen, if her face was blue. After calming her daughter, Helen explained as they looked in a mirror that Sharon's face was not blue no matter what anyone else said. Helen reminded her that the other girl's opinion was not true and was said to get a laugh at Sharon's expense. She advised her daughter to reject the message and, next time, to look in the mirror herself when someone made a comment about her.

How do we come to know who we are? Although various experiences influence how we come to understand ourselves, messages received from family, peers, teachers, other adults and the media have a major impact on our self-concept.

Messages have power. They can influence our thinking, feelings and actions. Sometimes the influence is direct and intentional; sometimes it's indirect and unplanned. Messages can be in our Best Interest or our Worst Interest.

The story *Chicken Little* offers a great example of the power of messages. When an acorn falls on Chicken Little's head, she tells her friends that the sky is falling. They believe the false message and become frantic. Her friends don't check her emotionally delivered message with any facts or their own experiences. Without questioning, they take her message in and accept it as their own fate.

VALIDITY AND INTERPRETATION

Two important aspects of messages are validity and interpretation:

> **Validity** is whether the message is true or false.

> **Interpretation** is whether we **believe** the message is true or false.

Sharon's story shows how the validity and interpretation of each message creates four possibilities:

FOUR MESSAGE POSSIBILITIES	
1. True messages can be interpreted as True.	Helen says Sharon's face is normal and Sharon believes her mother.
2. True messages can be interpreted as False.	Helen says Sharon's face is normal but Sharon does not believe her.
3. False messages can be interpeted as True.	Sharon is told her face is blue and she believes it.
4. False messages can be interpreted as False.	Sharon is told her face is blue but does not believe it.

In the children's tale *The Ugly Duckling*, the 'duckling' hatched in the nest was not a duck at all but a misplaced baby swan. The message this 'duckling' heard and believed from other ducks was that it was ugly. Later discovering that he looked and swam like a swan, the 'duckling' rejected the false 'ugly' message.

Bottom 80 thinkers often misinterpret messages they receive. This affects their Frame negatively. Because Top 20 thinkers more accurately interpret true messages as true and false messages as false, their Frame produces more positive results.

BELIEFS ACTIVATE POTENTIAL

Being able to accurately interpret messages is a valuable Top 20 Parenting tool. For ourselves and our children, messages impact who we think we are and what we can do. **The messages we interpret as true become our beliefs about ourselves.** True messages that become our beliefs help us develop our potential. False messages that become our beliefs block our potential. Just as water and energy from the sun activate the potential in a seed, beliefs activate potential in a person.

In the beloved children's book *The Little Engine that Could*, the Little Blue Engine is asked to pull the long train over the mountain to children on the other side. Even though she's a small engine previously only used for switching trains, she believes she can do it. "I think I can...I think I can...I think I can" is the message she tells herself as she attempts this new task. The Little Engine's full potential is influenced by whether she believes she can only be used for switching trains or has the strength to accomplish larger feats.

> "Whether you think you can do a thing or you think you can't do a thing, you're right."
>
> –Henry Ford

HANGOUTS

Where do we 'hang out'? We're not talking about physical hangouts, but mental and emotional hangouts. Let's consider two important hangouts that relate to messages.

Core -- Our True Self: The very first hangout is our Core. This is where our True Self resides. We can think of our Core as what's inside a seed: its true identity, worth, purpose and potential. What's inside our Core is our true identity, worth, purpose and potential.

Seeds have worth because of what they are and what they will become. Likewise, **our children, even as newborn babies who cannot offer or do anything of value, have inherent worth because of who they are.**

An apple seed has the specific purpose of becoming a tree that produces apples. **Our children's specific purpose is to become uniquely their True Self.** Purpose is about being what we are meant to be. That might mean not being what mom wants (a concert violinist) or what dad wants (a basketball star). Just as the purpose of an apple seed is not to become an orange tree or a rosebush, neither is our children's purpose to become anyone other than who they are.

> "When I get to the other life, I will not be asked, 'Why were you not Moses?' I will be asked, 'Why were you not Zusye?'"
>
> –Rabbi Zusye

Whereas an apple might admire the color of an orange or the scent of a rose, it will frustrate itself trying to become an orange or a rose. Likewise, we might admire a quality in another person, but we will be frustrated if we are not our True Self.

Circumference -- The Land of Other People: Once born, we begin hanging out in a second place: the Circumference or Land of Other People. The Land of Other People is full of wonderful and dangerous things that often take the form of:

OPOs = Other People's Opinions

OPEs = Other People's Expectations

OPAs = Other People's Agendas

Other People's Opinions: While it's important to keep open to feedback from others because it can help us see what we need to see, **OPOs are not always in our Best Interest and can limit us.** Bottom 80s often let OPOs determine their decisions and actions without analyzing whether the OPOs are in their Best Interest. Although Top 20s care about OPOs, they stay detached while analyzing whether they are in their Best Interest. Consequently, Top 20s deflect opinions that do not nurture their Core.

Other People's Expectations: Other people have expectations of what we should do or say, wear or drive, like or dislike, or be in the future. Some of these expectations might be worth striving for. However, some OPEs may not be in our Best Interest or in harmony with our Core. **Our future should be charted by our own goals stemming from our Core and not OPEs.** Bottom 80s can be imprisoned by the expectations of others. Top 20s are open to hearing the expectations of others, but freely reject them if they are not in keeping with their Core or in their Best Interest.

Other People's Agendas: Other people will have agendas for us about how they think things should happen. It is good to be mindful of how other people are approaching an event or situation. Cooperation and empathy are important. However, **OPAs may not be in our Best Interest and may conflict with our Core.** Our own values and intentions ought to determine our actions. Whereas Bottom 80s organize their lives according to the agendas of others, Top 20s chart their own course in keeping with their Core and Best Interest while respecting the agendas of others.

What's dangerous about the Circumference? If we pay lots of attention to OPOs, OPEs and OPAs, we can forget our Core identity, worth and purpose. Children are especially vulnerable to the influences of messages from other people since they lack awareness of their Core.

If we hang out exclusively on the Circumference, we forget our Core and true purpose. Instead of becoming our True Self, we strive to **please other people.** Pleasing other people is fine as long as we don't forget our Core and sacrifice our True Self. However, if we routinely please other people by ignoring our own opinions, expectations and agendas, we will experience the frustration that comes from denying our True Self. We want our children to become resilient teenagers capable of resisting the dangers of outside opinions.

What's wonderful about the Circumference? Sometimes the OPOs, OPEs and OPAs actually connect us to our Core. Others may want us to think, act or be according to our True Self. By believing in and reminding us of our identity, worth and purpose, they help us awaken our potential.

The movie *Lion King* offers a great example of this. The young lion Simba holds the false belief that he is responsible for his father's death. Steeped in guilt, he rejects his role as king and leaves his homeland. While living off by himself, he meets Rafiki, a monkey who sees the true identity and potential of Simba and guides him back to his True Self.

PARENTAL MESSAGES SUPPORTING THE CORE

Every person needs someone who believes in her worth and value as a human being, someone who fuels the Core with positive messages. Even if others are telling a child that she is worthless, it takes only one meaningful adult in a child's life to shore up her self-concept and protect Core messages.

Children receive a constant flow of messages from parents, relatives, other caregivers and the media. "You clumsy kid" is a message that can be absorbed as a belief just as surely as "I'm so proud of you."

We must think carefully about what we want children to believe about themselves and consistently send messages that will form those beliefs.

Parents can help children stay connected to what is embedded in their Core by sending powerful messages. Comments like, "I'm glad you're my daughter; you make me smile everyday" or "You are learning to build your block tower higher and higher each day" help children know their worth and that we believe they are capable and have loads of potential. **Our belief will activate their potential.**

As our children grow up they will spend more time hanging out in the Land of OP. We need to set aside time, such as bedtime, before going out the door each morning or on special occasions like a child's birthday, to reinforce Core messages. Strengthening Core messages daily gives balance to the messages that they will hear from others. No matter what messages he might someday hear from the playground bully, a child can go back to his Core and think, "I'm a valuable person. I have great worth and potential."

> "Thoughts, like fleas, jump from man to man. But they don't bite everybody."
> **Stanislaw Lec**

Parents also have the responsibility to help children interpret and deflect the negative messages they receive from the Land of OP. Role playing about how to respond to insults, opinions and comments in certain situations provides concrete learning for how to deal with messages that are not in a child's Best Interest. Children can be taught to compare messages with their own Core self-concept: Is this a true message or not? Should I accept this message or reject it?

OUR MESSAGES AND BELIEFS FORM OUR CHILDREN'S FUTURE

Helen Keller overcame many obstacles in life, including being blind and deaf, to make incredible contributions to society. Before her teacher, Ann Sullivan, arrived, young Helen was creating a very different and desolate future for herself. But Ann believed in Helen's potential until Helen could believe it for herself. Ann's belief transformed Helen's life.

Sometimes people can't see for themselves the absolute radiance of their potential. We can help them to see it by believing in them first. The message we offer is, "I will believe in this for you until you can see it for yourself." This is how parents can develop potential in children. For example, a two-year-old child is not technically reading, but is showing interest in books. Knowing that interest in books will result in reading in the future, an astute parent can tell the two-year-old that she is a great reader now. **We help form our children's future by what we believe about them.**

73

REJECTING HARMFUL MESSAGES

By securely knowing about ourselves and remaining true to our Core, we can analyze the barrage of messages coming at us and decide which messages are in harmony with our Best Interest. Top 20s look to their Core to decide about messages. Bottom 80s are more likely to make choices contrary to their Best Interest by accepting false messages and rejecting true messages about their identity, worth and purpose.

We can think of a burning match as a metaphor for harmful messages and beliefs. Imagine holding on to a match until it burned us. Sometimes we hold on to painful messages that burn us, forgetting that we have a choice to let go. As Top 20 Parents we want to teach our children to reject harmful or self-limiting messages as soon as possible.

DEVELOPMENTAL NEWS FLASH!!!

• **Cognitive development in young children is still immature.** They have trouble discerning the difference between true or false and real events and imagination. Because children at first believe all messages are true, they are extremely vulnerable to the impact of messages. Until they have enough life experience to trust themselves, our youngest children will second-guess what they thought they knew when faced with a new message. For example, an eight-year-old will know that a dog is a dog, even though he hears someone say it is a cat. A toddler, however, may call the dog a cat because he hears someone else call the dog a cat.

• **A young child's initial concept of self is largely developed through interaction with caregivers.** Little ones get their messages about themselves from their caregivers. They value and believe the opinions of these significant people. If a child is told she is stupid, she will tend to think it is true. Children depend on people closest to them to validate and interpret messages. The closer the relationship, the more weight given the messages and opinions.

TRUE TALES

Remember little Sharon who was told she had a blue face? She learned to look to her True Self when confronted with negative messages. Later in high school, a math teacher told her that girls were not good at math and that he would not, therefore, take the time to help her when she didn't understand a lesson. Although her math grade was very low, his message didn't fit her Core image of herself that she could improve if she worked at it. Rejecting his opinion, Sharon worked with a tutor from the math club and her grade improved dramatically.

The most important discovery we can make in our life is to discover WHO WE ARE.
The most important people in our life are those who help us discover WHO WE ARE.
The most important thing we can do for our children is help them discover WHO THEY ARE.

TIME FOR ACTION!

For Parents to Do:

1. Think about negative messages from others, including OPOs, OPEs, and OPAs, that have influenced your life. Which false messages have you interpreted as true? What messages have you been holding onto for a lifetime?

2. Think of three people who truly value you for your True Self. How have these people nurtured your Core?

3. How often do you compare your parenting with that of others? Is this helpful or does it result in a negative message?

4. Think of how often you compare your child with other children. How does this influence your messages to your child?

To Do with Your Child:

1. Watch how your child approaches new activities and notice when he says or indicates "I can" or "I can't." What is his behavior saying about his Core?

2. Notice how children relay positive and negative messages to each other. How does your child respond to positive and negative messages?

3. Give your child at least one positive message each day. Be aware of nonverbal negative messages you may be giving her such as sighs, stern looks and gestures.

4. Read books to your child (see Appendix C, p. 124) that demonstrate lessons about messages.

5. Talk to your child about messages in the media. What might the messages from TV commercials or shows be telling her to believe about herself. What are they telling her to think, say, do or wear?

CHAPTER 13

Mistake Making
Oops! Now What?

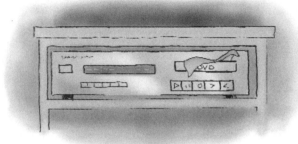

*"There is much to be said for failure.
It is more interesting than success."*
—Max Beerbohm

Dan and Jenny settled in to watch a movie after a long day caring for their busy toddlers. Imagine their frustration when the DVD would not go into the player. Upon closer inspection, they discovered fruit snacks jammed into the machine. "This is the worst thing those boys have done yet!" cried Jenny angrily. "Now they broke the DVD player."

We've seen how positive and negative messages influence adults and children. What and how parents communicate about mistakes provides powerful messages to their children. Top 20 Parents are aware of how they feel about their own mistakes and how they respond to their children's mistakes.

When we make mistakes we often get responses from other people. Positive responses include forgiving, understanding, helping and supporting. More common, however, are negative reactions:

- laughing
- judging
- yelling
- shaming

- showing anger
- teasing
- isolating
- punishing

- being disappointed
- withdrawing affection
- bringing it up again
- giving disapproving looks

If these are the reactions we get when we make a mistake, the message is loud and clear, "YOU BETTER NOT MAKE A MISTAKE." However, as human beings we are going to make mistakes. What we hear as messages about our mistakes can influence our beliefs about ourselves and mistake making. These in turn will affect how we communicate with our children.

OUR RESPONSES TO MISTAKES

As you might expect, we will treat mistakes differently depending on whether we are in a Top 20 or Bottom 80% state of mind. Following are four common Bottom 80 reactions.

DENIAL — We cover up the mistake or pretend it didn't happen. If someone else brings it up, we deny it or get defensive.

BLAME — We acknowledge the mistake but blame someone else for it: "He did it" or " She made me do it." In blaming others we avoid responsibility.

JUSTIFY — We admit to the mistake but give reasons for our actions to avoid negative reactions from others: "I didn't get the bills paid on time because I was helping the kids with their homework."

DWELL — We focus on nothing else but the mistake and allow the mistake to define us: "I'm so stupid. I never do anything right. I'll never be able to get over this."

These are considered Bottom 80 reactions because they do not lead to learning the lesson life intends for us to get from a mistake. When we don't get the lesson, we are more likely to repeat the mistake. As we know, the consequences for repeated mistakes become more and more severe.

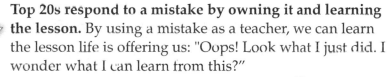

Top 20s respond to a mistake by owning it and learning the lesson. By using a mistake as a teacher, we can learn the lesson life is offering us: "Oops! Look what I just did. I wonder what I can learn from this?"

> "Failure is the opportunity to begin again more intelligently."
> –Henry Ford

MESSAGES ABOUT MISTAKES

Parents can have unrealistic expectations about what young children can do and label as mistakes behaviors that are really quite typical for a child's developmental age. Young children can be clumsy, slow, irritating and noisy. Although they may do this repeatedly, these behaviors are what we would expect of young children as they develop. Parents who punish a child for what is age appropriate behavior misunderstand a child's normal development and needs.

The messages parents send about mistakes leaves a powerful mental and emotional imprint on children. Top 20 Parents help their children learn positive lessons from mistakes. Bottom 80 Parents pass on negative messages when their children make mistakes.

A BOTTOM 80 PARENTAL REACTION:

Do you know what you boys have done?

You've broken a very expensive machine!

Now stay in your room.

And don't touch anything in the house again.

Bottom 80 Lessons about Mistake Making: If children are talked to in this fashion, what are the likely messages they get from making mistakes?

1. **You can't do anything right.** If a parent's immediate reaction is about failure, then a child's value and worth will be diminished. She will come to believe, "I'm not good enough."

2. **Avoid trying things because you might make a mistake.** When children get this message, their natural curiosity begins to shut down. They will avoid taking healthy risks that lead to growth and learning.

3. **The lesson is in the punishment.** If kids have learned that mistakes require punishment, they will fear mistakes and learn to lie, blame and deny in order to avoid embarrassment or punishment.

A TOP 20 PARENTAL RESPONSE:

Dan remembered something he had heard from the early childhood teacher.

> Dan: "Toddlers have a developmental urge to stuff things into small places to learn about volume."
>
> Jenny: "I didn't realize that. Hmmm, tomorrow let's give them containers for stuffing."
>
> Dan: "And let's help them clean up the DVD player."
>
> Jenny: "Yeah and put the DVD player out of their reach."

Top 20 Lessons about Mistake Making: If we want our children to not fear mistakes and continually grow from life experiences, some crucial messages need to be communicated when they make mistakes.

1. **You are more important than the mistake.** If a parent's immediate concern is for the child's well-being and safety, then the child's value and worth will be reinforced.

2. **Help is available when you make a mistake.** One of our purposes as parents is to help our children when they experience difficulties. It is not our responsibility to take care of the entire problem and clean up the mess for them, but to support our kids in making things better.

> "Learning that we are capable of making up for a mistake or an accident is very important to the development of self-esteem."
>
> –Magda Gerber

3. **Things can be made better after a mistake.** When we make a mistake, we're responsible for fixing things or cleaning up the mess.

4. **Lessons are in the mistake.** Life intends for parents and children to learn important lessons from the mistakes they make.

5. **Mistakes are wonderful**. Because many wonderful things can be learned from mistakes, they are to be valued and not avoided.

Children need to experience mistakes in such a way that they know that **failure is an event, not a person.** Top 20 Parents communicate messages to their children that failure is just an event from which we can benefit. Failure should not be a label for who a child is but for what he has done.

DEVELOPMENTAL NEWS FLASH!

Since the messages children receive from mistake making impact their growth, parents need to keep development in mind when they respond to their children's behavior.

• **Young children are uncoordinated.** Kids will make many mistakes because they are clumsy. They have not fully mastered the coordination of their bodies and muscles.

• **The logic of young children is faulty.** Because they are cognitively immature, young children will get mixed up in their thinking about concepts and solutions. For example, a child may repeatedly try to jam a puzzle piece into the wrong place. She may misjudge her own ability and carry a bucket that is clearly too heavy for her, thereby spilling the contents.

• **Young children have fewer inhibitions about their behaviors.** They may pick their noses in public, unaware of the inappropriateness of that action. They may say things that are inappropriate to adults: "Hey, lady, you've got a lot of wrinkles!"

• **Young children cannot use memory reliably to make connections.** Their brains are not yet mature enough for learning by thinking about a past event. Therefore, giving a young child a Time Out to 'think about what you've done' will often be useless.

• **Young children are not able to connect cause and effect reliably.** Because of development, children need to be guided to see the connections between their behaviors and their responsibility. They cannot reliably process past errors and make improvements for 'Next Time'.

• **Young children learn best through experimentation, exploration and experiencing new things.** They are curious problem solvers and enthusiastic explorers who can create messes and court danger unaware of the consequences of their behaviors.

THE BIG LEARNING OUTSIDE OUR COMFORT ZONE

Because it's easy for us to do things **inside** our Comfort Zone, we may be reluctant to try things **outside** our Comfort Zone.

Thomas Edison failed hundreds of times before he found a workable filament for the light bulb. Like Edison, children need to go through mistakes if they are going to get Big Learning. But, if we teach them to fear mistakes, they'll only hang out in the safety of their Comfort Zone.

Top 20 Kids move outside their Comfort Zone to take healthy risks and learn from mistakes. The more they do it, the more they learn and the easier it gets. As a result, Top 20 Kids succeed at higher and higher levels.

A.C.T.

Mistakes will happen in life. How we A.C.T. to our own mistakes and the mistakes of our children will send them powerful messages and lessons that will result in their learning from or fearing mistakes and venturing out or staying locked inside their Comfort Zone.

A is **Awareness.** As parents, we need to be Aware of our beliefs about ourselves as mistake makers. These beliefs have come from the messages from others when we have made mistakes. **Awareness of our beliefs is critical because those beliefs will activate our reactions or responses when our children make mistakes.**

C is **Conscious Choice.** Top 20 Parents make two Conscious Choices: how they want to respond when they make a mistake and when their children make a mistake. A phrase that can be helpful when we make a mistake is: "Oops, look what I just did. I wonder what I can learn from this." This phrase focuses us on taking responsibility for the mistake and seeking the lesson we need to learn. A Conscious Choice phrase we can use when our children make a mistake is: "What can we learn from this?"

T is **Talking.** Top 20 Parents talk about their own mistake making with their children. For example, a mother during dinner might say to her family, "I made a mistake at work today. I'd like to share it with you. Maybe you can help me learn everything I can from that mistake." In this way, parents demonstrate to children that mistakes are valuable life experiences not to be hidden or denied.

Our children need us to help them learn from mistakes. If we can respond to their mistake making experiences as Top 20 Parents, we will launch our children on a life-long journey of learning and growing as Top 20 Kids.

How do children learn to correct their mistakes?
By watching how you correct yours.
How do children learn to overcome their failures?
By watching how your overcome yours.
How do children learn to treat themselves with forgiveness?
By watching you forgive yourself.
Therefore, your mistakes and your failures are blessings,
opportunities for the best in parenting.

–Lao Tzu Tao Te Ching,
Adapted by William Martin

TIME FOR ACTION!

For Parents to Do:

1. What messages or lessons about mistakes did you get growing up?

2. How do you handle your own mistakes now? What changes, if any, do you want to make in thinking about your own mistakes?

3. What messages about mistake making do you want to communicate to your child?

4. Talk with your family about a mistake you have made and invite them to help you learn the lessons embedded in that experience.

To Do with Your Child:

1. Keep track of actions that your child views as mistakes (spilling milk, breaking a toy) and to which he reacts negatively.

2. Role-play mistake making with your child and practice the phrase: "Oops. Look what I just did. I wonder what I can learn from this."

3. Help your child learn valuable lessons from mistakes instead of denying, blaming, justifying or dwelling. Discuss solutions and prevention for 'Next Time'.

4. Read to your child books (see Appendix C, p. 124) that address mistake making.

CHAPTER 14

Reducing Negativity
Family Safety Alert:
Tornadoes and Thought Circles

*"The child doesn't have the tantrum...
the tantrum has the child."*

–Magda Gerber

When Matt came home after work, the first words out of his mouth were, "When's supper?" His wife gave him a withering look that said she didn't appreciate the question. He responded stormily, "What? You couldn't get to it again today? Like I should make supper after the day that I had? The boss is squeezing me dry. And I sure don't appreciate the racket the boys are making either." Matt bellowed to the kids in the basement, "Hey, knock it off or I'll come down and make you be quiet."

When his daughter walked through the kitchen, he shifted his tirade to her, "Not so fast, missy. I remember asking you to clean up your room. I'm sure it's not done because you never listen to me. Now get up there and don't come down until supper....whenever that is." His daughter stomped off in a huff as Matt concluded with a dig, "This house is a mess. I don't even know where to sit down. I'll be in the garage until something right happens for a change."

Ever witness a tornado? In the movie 'Twister' the storm sends a cow, fence and pickup truck flying across the road. The destructive force of a tornado has power over everything in its path. This is what the 'weather' can be like Below the Line -- volatile, chaotic and scary. The story describes how Matt's individual tantrum became a family tornado event.

When we are thinking Below the Line, the conditions are always right for social **Tornadoes** or individual **Thought Circles.** Top 20 Parents know about these and how they get formed.

TORNADOES OF NEGATIVITY

A Tornado is the awesome power of social influence towards negativity. Tornadoes tend to occur when we are communicating Below the Line. Because our negativity is contagious, others can be drawn into our destructive energy. As others are drawn into the Tornado, it becomes more and more intense. It seems to take on a life of its own while making it difficult for its participants to escape. Just as Matt's negative tantrum pulled in the rest of his family, a child's tantrum has the power to draw in parents.

A group phenomenon of human behavior can be called '**trash, slash and bash'.** This occurs when saying negative things to belong to a group becomes the dominant way people in the group communicate. 'Trash, slash and bash' communication quickly spirals because it has the negative energy of many people. Indicators of 'trash, slash, and bash' conversation are blaming or talking negatively about someone who is not present.

It is hard to resist the pressure of adding a negative comment when communicating in a negative social atmosphere. Children, not knowing that there are other ways to communicate, will believe that negativity is what is required of them.

TORNADOES IN OUR FAMILY

Top 20 Parents minimize negativity and prevent their families from being torn up by Tornadoes. We can protect our family from devastating social storms by the following:

1. **Identify the Tornado as such.** If we are approaching a situation where a Tornado has started, we can identify it for the whole family's awareness: "Uh oh, sounds like there's a Tornado going on here."

2. **Identify family members who are Tornado starters.** Temperament can play a big role in starting Tornadoes for both children and adults. The temperament traits that can spawn tornadoes are a negative first response to events, mood, intensity and a persistence in holding on to negativity. It's helpful if we are aware of the temperament of family members, know who's Above or Below the Line and what triggers individual family members.

3. **Knowing child development is important for understanding our child's behaviors and recognizing which strategies will de-escalate Tornadoes.** For example, two-year-olds tend to have numerous temper tantrums. Because they are also very distractible, starting a new and exciting activity can rob a Tornado of strength.

4. **Forecast Tornadoes.** Just like the Weather Channel on TV, it's possible to predict stormy weather in the family. We can do this by paying attention to Tornado watches, warnings and touchdowns. Let's see how these events look in families.

   Tornado Watch: Conditions are right for producing Tornadoes.
   Be aware of where Tornado Watches occur in family life.
   - mornings when everyone needs to be somewhere on time
   - when a family member is BTL
   - dinner time or bed time
   - developmental transitions (terrible twos, potty training)
   - temperament clashes between family members (tired parent and active kid; social parent and shy kid)

   Tornado Warning: A funnel cloud has actually been sighted.
   The first sign of an actual Tornado almost always occurs when something or someone is spoken of in a negative way.
   - "I hate it when we have lasagna."
   - "Get your shoes. You make me late for work every day!"
   - "Mom, he's looking at me funny. Make him stop it."

Tornado Touchdown: The Tornado has hit the ground.

Before you know it you have been pulled in and have become a participant. The following three examples illustrate Tornado Touchdowns.

"I see a tornado".

- •. Husband says, "Why is dinner always late?" Wife reacts, "Don't complain to me. I have two screaming kids fighting and the laundry to fold."
- • Father says, "Get your shoes on." Son yells, "No, I won't," as he throws his shoes under the bed, then runs away.
- • Daughter says, "Mom, my brother's looking at me funny." Mother yells to son, "Stop looking at her right now! I don't care if she's poking you."

5. Listen without taking it to heart. Learn the difference between listening to what someone is saying and taking what they are saying to heart. It is possible to listen without agreeing. For example, a child might yell at a parent, "I hate you." Instead of taking this to heart and reacting by yelling back, a parent's calm response might be, "You don't have to like me but you DO have to hold my hand when we cross the street."

6. Respond by saying, "I hear you." We can weaken the Tornado by saying 'OK' or 'I hear you' or 'Life can be rough' without matching the negativity with our own downer comments. In this way we acknowledge the feelings of those in the Tornado without adding more negative energy.

"On the weekend I was in such a bad mood and it was catching on, dragging the whole family down. Once I noticed the Tornado and left my family to take a walk it was better. I could look at why I was Below the Line and what to do to get myself Above. It wasn't a great day but it sure was better after I stepped away for awhile."

–A stay-at-home Dad

7. Leave the Tornado scene. If a Tornado persists with its 'seek and destroy' mission, we may walk away from the situation. Going to another room briefly or starting a new activity can help. Declaring a quiet time or taking everyone to a new area of the house are also options.

8. Take more drastic measures. Tornadoes are extremely dangerous. If certain friends or groups are dominated by Tornadoes, we may need to take more drastic and courageous measures to protect ourselves or our family members. We may need to practice the followng three options.

E

Expanding our knowledge and support networks by:

• Making a goal to meet neighborhood families at the playground.
• Joining informal playgroups for Moms or Dads.
• Being a friend to other families in need.
• Increasing our understanding of development and other family related topics by reading or taking a parenting class.

L

Limiting our time in Tornado situations by:

• Limiting time with a negative uncle, sister-in-law or neighbor.
• Changing schedules or habits. If our child has a regular whine session in the car after being picked up from daycare, we can give him a snack as we get him into the carseat and introduce a different topic before he launches into a Tornado.
• Alerting our family when conditions are right for Tornado activity. For example, a parent could say, "Things don't go well when we try to play games together before naptime. Let's try something new. We'll have quiet reading time before nap. You look at books in your room and I will read my magazine in the other room."

T

Terminating the relationship when:

• We have tried talking about the problem or being a positive influence, but it is not getting any better.
• A relationship is not in our Best Interest.

When handling the difficult task of terminating a relationship, try to avoid blaming or accusing the other person.

Although we cannot terminate our relationship with our children, at times we may need to help them limit or terminate their relationship with other kids.

Trying to eliminate Tornadoes from our life doesn't mean we should never share negative feelings with friends or family members. Eliminating Tornadoes is not about eliminating emotions. It's healthy to share feelings and concerns with others. It's just that when we're Below the Line we need to express feelings and concerns in ways that don't create Tornadoes that hurt others or draw them in.

THOUGHT CIRCLES

Thought Circles occur when one thought leads quickly to another and another like a snow ball getting larger as it rolls down hill. Thought Circles move beyond facts to imaginary thoughts. As such they create feelings of worry, self-doubt and anger that produce grudges and judgment. These feelings and actions thrive Below the Line and are not in our Best Interest.

At 2:00 a.m., Lizabeta's Thought Circle may go something like this:

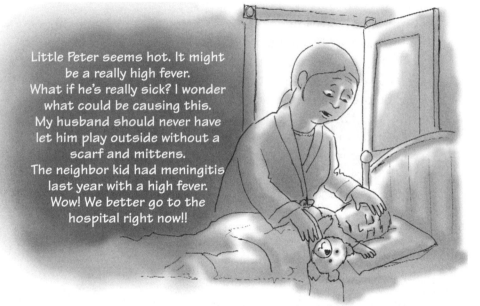

Little Peter seems hot. It might be a really high fever.
What if he's really sick? I wonder what could be causing this.
My husband should never have let him play outside without a scarf and mittens.
The neighbor kid had meningitis last year with a high fever.
Wow! We better go to the hospital right now!!

After rushing the child to the hospital, Peter is diagnosed with a mild ear infection. Only then does Lizabeta remember that her older children also had fevers with their ear infections.

Although Thought Circles are experienced in the mind of one person, they have enough power to affect those nearby. In addition, individual Thought Circles easily contribute to group Tornadoes.

THE WORRY THOUGHT CIRCLE

Thought Circles are the anatomy of worry. Lizabeta's worry formed because she allowed her thoughts to jump to conclusions and imagine the worst possible outcome.

Worry = Fact + Jumping to worst possible outcome

It only takes seconds for a Thought Circle to go from the first thought to the tenth thought. The sooner we realize we are having a Thought Circle the easier it is to stop it. It would have been in Lizabeta's Best Interest to handle the situation differently: "My child is hot. What could be causing this? Wait, this could be the start of a Thought Circle. I know I'm tired so I better stop and think. I better gather some facts. I'll take Peter's temperature first and ask him questions about what hurts." By gathering facts Lizabeta would delay her judgment from being clouded by imagination and make a more accurate diagnosis of the problem.

"I can't believe someone I love so much can make me so mad!"

–A Parent

THE ANGRY THOUGHT CIRCLE

Anger is a common emotion in family life. Often this anger flows from a Thought Circle that pulls us Below the Line where our reactions to our child's behaviors will not be in anyone's Best Interest.

This cartoon illustrates the anatomy of anger. In just one minute this Angry Thought Circle cost the mother:

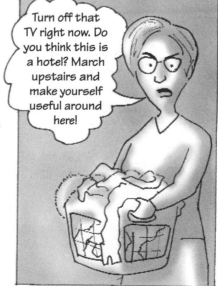

- Enjoyable thoughts of her child
- Pleasant time spent with her child
- A positive deposit into the Trust Fund
- An opportunity to teach about chores and responsibility in a positive way

All of these opportunities are lost, not because the child was intentionally trying to make the mother's life miserable, but because of the mother's own Angry Thought Circle.

STOP THOUGHT CIRCLES IN THEIR TRACKS

One simple way to stop Thought Circles is to use the 'Not Now' technique. When we become aware of a Thought Circle, we can say: "Stop. This is a Thought Circle. Not now." This prevents the Thought Circle from gaining momentum and pulling us further Below the Line.

Another strategy is the Parking Lot. Sometimes the concern that initiates a Thought Circle needs to be seriously considered. If we're unable to give a problem or situation the attention it may require at the time, we can put that issue in our mental Parking Lot and make an appointment with ourselves to deal with it later. Then we can focus on whatever is in the present moment. By not spending the day caught up in a Thought Circle falling further Below the Line, we'll be better able to approach the situation later by being Above the Line.

Using 'Not Now' or putting things in the mental Parking Lot are ways of taking control of our life. They are ways of creating a better experience for ourselves by dealing with concerns when we are best able to do so.

DEVELOPMENTAL NEWS FLASH!!!

As a parent works to control the family 'weather', it will be helpful to know how development affects the thinking of young children.

• **Young children are emotionally immature.** We want young children to learn to recognize emotions in others. We also want them to know that some emotional situations, like Tornadoes, are toxic and should not be mimicked or absorbed. Young children need our coaching on how to recognize and deflect negative emotions.

• **The logic of young children is faulty.** They can get very upset about things that seem irrational to us. The illogical connections of cause and effect can quickly lead young children to Thought Circles. For example, they might fear the toilet flushing because it will swallow them or they may believe that Mom got sick because they didn't clean up their toys.

BRAIN POWER

We wouldn't let our legs take us somewhere that we didn't want to go, but we often let our brain and its thoughts take us where we don't really want to be. As human beings we have the power to make our brain work for us and not be led into negativity by Tornadoes or into anger or worry by Thought Circles. These things damage the quality of our lives, relationships and experiences.

All Top 20 Parenting strategies for stormy BTL weather of Tornadoes and Thought Circles invite us to focus on our thinking. If we want to experience something better, we first need to be more aware of and govern our thinking. Being aware of our thoughts, their effects on actions and how to change our thinking gives us great power to be the authors of our own lives and not characters in someone else's story.

For Parents to Do:

1. Observe your family for warning signs of Tornadoes of Negativity. Try to change the situation before a Tornado can form.

2. Consider the negative influences in your social circles. Do you need to expand, limit or terminate any influences?

3. Observe when you take someone's negative comments to heart. Practice listening without getting pulled in emotionally to a Tornado.

4. Recall a recent Thought Circle. Was it worry or anger that gave it energy? Imagine being in that Thought Circle now and practice either 'Not Now' or the Parking Lot.

To Do with Your Child:

1. Observe when your child is about to create a Tornado. Point out the warning signs to her. Engage her in learning to change the situation and thinking for herself.

2. Consider negative influences (like TV) in your child's environment. Talk to your child about necessary changes.

3. Observe for anger or worry Thought Circles developing in your child. As you help him understand accurate cause and effect, you can also help him use strategies like 'Not Now' and the Parking Lot to keep the negative impact of Thought Circles to a minimum.

CHAPTER 15

Listening
"Huh? What Were You Saying?"

"What we've got here is failure to communicate."
–Cool Hand Luke

"I don't want you to go outside today," yelled Nina upstairs to her children. "It's too cold." Soon the children were putting on their boots and snow gear. "What are you doing?" asked Nina confused. "I said that you weren't going outside."

"But we thought you said, 'Go outside today'. That's what we heard." Now disappointed, the children began fighting with each other.

In a few minutes Nina's husband came through the kitchen, "So, Nina, what's this about you having a cold?" With disgust Nina explained, "No. I was telling the kids that it was too cold to play outside today." "Oops," said her husband, "While I was reading the paper I thought I heard you say you were coming down with a cold. So I canceled our dinner reservations for tonight. You always tell me I don't listen to you when you say you're not feeling like going out. So I thought you'd want me to cancel."

What is probably responsible for more relationship problems than anything else is poor communication. Poor communication is usually caused by poor listening.

Listening is powerful. Although almost everyone has the potential to listen, only a few people develop that ability. Top 20s know that the ability to truly listen will benefit them in five major ways:

1. **Learning:** Listening is a primary channel through which learning in school, at work and in life takes place.

2. **Creating understanding:** True listening enables us to understand. Failure to listen creates misunderstandings.

3. **Solving problems:** Solving problems, especially problems between people, requires openness to learning and listening to understand. As in the introductory story, many problems can be made worse by a failure to truly listen.

4. **Communicating 'You matter':** When we sincerely listen to understand another person, we communicate to her that she matters. Whether intentional or not, our failure to listen results in her feeling like she does not matter. As such, listening is a powerful tool by which we create trust in relationships.

5. **Being aware of self:** We have our own inner voice that expresses our needs, dreams, feelings and wisdom. Being aware of this voice enables us to live more fruitful and meaningful lives.

For these reasons, Top 20s value listening and practice to improve their listening skills. Bottom 80s assume they are listening all the time. Nina's children and husband thought they were listening, but they were mistaken.

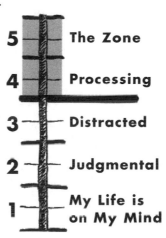

By being aware of five different levels of listening, we will be able to make choices resulting in more effective listening.

LEVEL 1: MY LIFE ON MY MIND

We're in the first level of listening when we're focused on our own life and what we've got going on. When we're listening with My Life on My Mind, we're really listening only to ourselves. If we are in this level as a parent, we are not really listening to our children. In order for them to get our attention, they may escalate annoying and whining behaviors.

> "What I learned about listening opened my eyes. No wonder kids nag and whine. They know we aren't listening to them, but we expect them to listen to us."
>
> –A Parent

Examples: "I wonder if we will be able to make the mortgage payment this month?"

"There are so many things to do before Joey's birthday party."

LEVEL 2: JUDGMENTAL

We sometimes visit a town called Judgmentville, a small-minded place with a huge population. Listening at this level includes:

- jumping to conclusions
- interrupting or finishing another's sentences

- evaluating self or others
- overreacting
- agreeing or disagreeing

Parents make judgments about children:

> "Why bother explaining. They never listen."
> "Kids are brats. They're always interrupting."

When children are judged, they feel disrespected and devalued.

Parents also make judgments of themselves:

> "I can't seem to control these kids. I'll never be a good parent."
> "My brother's kids never act like this. What's wrong with me?"

LEVEL 3: DISTRACTED

We are in Level 3 when our attention is distracted by something in the environment, such as the TV, another person walking by or a buzzing fly. A distracted parent might begin listening to a child but then lose attention to a song on the radio, what the child is fiddling with, or a ringing phone.

LEVEL 4: PROCESSING

Processing may begin by truly listening but then goes off to analyzing, memorizing or synthesizing what is being said. We are often in this level when we are listening to someone expressing a problem. Long before we fully understand the problem, we engage in solving the problem.

Processing can also occur while a parent is reading this book. A parent may be very engaged in the material he is reading but immediately begin thinking about how it can be applied to family or work situations.

There is a place and a time for all four of these levels. However, these levels are not useful when we need to focus on something important in the present moment. At these times we will have a better experience or be more effective if we are able to be in the Zone.

LEVEL 5: THE ZONE

Being in the Zone occurs when our mind is quiet and calm. It's as if nothing is 'on' our mind. Rather, we are totally present to the moment and living in the NOW. Because we are not thinking about something else, our mind is like a sponge able to take in whatever the moment presents.

When we are in the other four levels, we are living in the past or the future. Our mind is like a soaked sponge unable to absorb whatever is taking place in the present moment. Parents who are able to listen in the Zone are able to listen accurately and then effectively respond to whatever needs attention.

GETTING TO THE ZONE

The average person spends 22 minutes out of every hour in Levels 1-4. With such a low level of effective listening, it's understandable that our communication is filled with misunderstandings, our learning is filled with gaps and our relationships struggle.

We're wired to be in the Zone and will automatically listen at this level if we merely stop being in the other levels. It's like cutting the sandbags from a hot air balloon. When that happens, the balloon automatically rises.

We can practice Top 20 listening in the Zone by doing the following:

1. Being aware when we are not in the Zone.

2. Saying 'Not now' whenever we have Life on My Mind, are Judging or being Distracted or Processing.

3. Using the Parking Lot. If something needs our attention, we can put it in our mental parking lot by setting a time to deal with it later and refocusing on what is going on in the moment.

Practicing these steps will help us live in the present moment and be better listeners. As such, we will enhance our learning, performing and relationships.

DEVELOPMENTAL NEWS FLASH!

Two questions parents ask on a regular basis are: "How do I get my child to listen to me?" and "How do I get my child to follow directions?" Although there are no magical secrets or quick fixes, parents can better understand how children develop the skills of listening and following directions. With a developmental understanding of language, we can use certain techniques to help our children develop listening skills.

• **Babies must learn which sounds to give their attention.** They do not consistently know how to discriminate which sounds to filter out and which to focus on in the environment. Babies also have differing states of alertness during their day that will dictate how much of outside sounds they 'get'. When babies have lots of experiences with sounds, talking and music, they will develop skill in discriminating sounds and language. Parents can enhance this skill development by talking to their baby, singing songs and exploring sounds together.

• **Young toddlers struggle to figure out on which words to focus.**

1. Their brains pay attention mostly to nouns and verbs but not other portions of language structure.

2. Negative words are unclear in sentences.

> "I told you not to bite Brian" is understood as "Bite Brian."
> "I don't want you to go outside" is understood as "Go outside."

3. Questions are difficult to process. A child's answers to questions (Are you hungry? Are you tired? Do you want to go to the park?) may not be accurate. A child may answer one way but mean something else. The question 'why' is extremely difficult for children to understand because it requires seeing the connection between cause and effect.

We can encourage growth in communication by talking with our children in specific ways that acknowledge the limitations of toddler language development:

> Match words with actions when giving commands: model picking up toys to show the concept of 'clean up'.

> Be specific when giving directions: 'Clean up' is not as good as 'Put the blue car on this shelf.'

> Ask 'What happened' or 'What were you trying to do' instead of 'Why'.

> Say what you want your child to DO instead of what you DON'T want your child to do: "Feet stay on the floor" instead of "Stop climbing" or "Walk on the sidewalk" instead of "Don't go in the street."

Narrate the actions of your child at play: "You are pushing the ball on the floor"; "You put five blocks together to make a tall tower."

Describe the objects of your child's play: "That ball is blue."

Get down to eye level and look your child in the eye while talking.

• **Preschoolers must learn how to process information.** They show listening ability but their communication and processing skills are incomplete. We get mad at children for not thinking like adults but their brains are not ready to process like an adult's. Here is what we know about preschoolers.

1. Attention span is short.

2. Memory is not fully developed, especially when not allowed to be 'hands on'.

3. Concrete thinking still gets in the way of talking about objects not present in the room. Preschoolers get confused about abstract concepts like time, honesty and responsibility.

4. Egocentrism will affect what information preschoolers are interested in talking about and remembering.

5. Only one element of a situation can be focused on at a time. A child cannot follow too many directions given at once.

The following activities will expand their processing skills:

  • Play games that strengthen memory and prolong attention span. Take a puzzle piece away to see if your child can guess what is missing. Use a timer to finish a puzzle.

  • Talk about things that are not in the room to develop abstract thought: talk about the zoo animals you saw yesterday or how loud a thunderstorm can be.

  • Relate information to the child's point of view and then help her see the points of view of other people: "You thought the kitten was little, but your brother was afraid because he thought it was so big."

  • Play sound discrimination games by guessing recorded sounds.

The ability to listen effectively is critical in school, work and relationships. The best thing we can do to raise Top 20 Kids who will succeed in these areas is to develop our own ability to listen. Modeling this powerful skill will not only be an example of how to listen in the Zone but will also communicate to children that they matter.

TIME FOR ACTION!

For Parents to Do:

1. Recall times when others did not listen to what you had to communicate.

2. In which level of listening do you spend most of your time? What gets in the way of your effective listening? Practice saying 'Not now' when you are aware that you have Life on My Mind, are Judgmental or Distracted.

To Do with Your Child:

1. Play 'Telephone' with your child, whispering a sentence or two back and forth. You can intentionally change the whispered words to see if he can discriminate the differences and remember what was originally whispered.

2. Ask your child to listen to some questions and answer with a 'yes', 'no' or 'maybe'. This activity gets children to listen and think at the same time. You can use the following questions and then make up your own:

    Can you pick up an elephant?   Does ice feel cold?

    Can you pick up a suitcase?   Do you wear a hat on your feet?

    Can you eat a chair?   Are you a girl? Are you a boy?

3. Try these strategies to help your child 'hear' your instructions and stay focused:

    • Make eye contact.

    • Keep instructions simple.

    • Tell children what they can do, not what they cannot do.

    • Use images and actions as well as words to communicate your message.

CHAPTER 16

Conflict Resolution
Heart-to-heart or Toe-to-toe

"There is no hope of joy except in human relations."
Saint-Exupery

Jakob, a tired and cranky dad, sends his children inside to play so he can cut the grass. When the children's indoor game of baseball breaks a cherished family vase, Sara, an equally tired and cranky mom, turns off the vacuum and yells at the children for making a mess in the living room. Soon Jakob and Sara are fighting.

"That's just great. My grandmother's vase can never be replaced!" says Jakob bitterly. "How can I win? If I play with the kids like they want me to and don't cut the grass, you call me lazy. Your problem is that you are always telling me what I'm doing wrong!"

"How can you win? Your problem is you always think of yourself first," retorts Sara, ready for battle. "You send the kids inside while I try to clean. They only make messes and never help. And with my new job I have less time to take care of the house. And another thing....."

The children slowly slink out of harm's way knowing that their parents will be fighting all night.

Conflicts are fights, struggles, battles and clashes that show disagreement or opposition. Even though these are things we do not desire, they are common experiences we all have. However, we will experience conflicts differently whether we are Bottom 80 or Top 20. Bottom 80s approach conflict Toe-to-toe and Top 20s approach it Heart-to-heart.

Conflict

Let's use the Frame: See-Feel-Do-Get to understand these two ways of dealing with conflict.

How do we SEE conflict?

Toe-Toe	Heart-Heart
This term comes from ancient battles when soldiers stood Toe-to-toe while attacking each other. When we are seeing conflict this way, we view each other as an adversary who we must defeat. Our goal is to win and cause the other person to lose. We focus on the issue or the 'thing' and lose sight of the relationship.	When we are operating Heart-to-heart, we are standing side by side and see each other as partners in an effort to discover what is mutually beneficial. Although the issue or 'thing' is still important, the relationship is of supreme importance.

The immediate issue between Jakob and Sara is the broken vase. Soon into their encounter they are no longer focusing on the vase but begin attacking each other. Besides the vase, what ultimately gets damaged in this exchange is their relationship and their children.

"He who strikes the first blow admits he's lost the argument."

–Chinese Proverb

What do we FEEL?

Toe-Toe	Heart-Heart
When we see ourselves in a losing situation, we will feel angry, defensive and frustrated.	When we are seeking to find what is mutually beneficial, we are willing, respectful, open-minded and cooperative.

Along with these feelings, Sara and Jakob feel unappreciated, defeated and insulted.

What do we DO?

Toe-Toe	Heart-Heart
When we see conflict as a Win-Lose battle and feel angry and defensive, our actions and behaviors will reflect our adversarial approach.	When we see conflict as a Win-Win opportunity and are respectful and cooperative, our actions will create what is beneficial for each other.

What we DO in conflict involves timing, listening and talking.

Timing	
As Bottom 80s we deal with the problem when we are Below the Line and ineffective.	As Top 20s we deal with the problem when we are Above the Line and more effective.

Jakob and Sara clash immediately after the vase breaks. They cannot reason with each other when they are so angry and Below the Line.

Listening	
Because Bottom 80s have Life on My Mind, are Distracted or Judgmental, they are not listening. Rather, they are interrupting and planning what to say while the other person is speaking.	Being in the Zone, Top 20s are listening to understand, listening for the point and listening to non-verbals. By doing so, they are creating respect and trust by communicating 'You matter'.

Jakob and Sara are unable to listen because they are too busy judging by pointing out flaws they see in each other.

Talking	
Bottom 80s respond with blame and 'You' statements. 'You' statements begin with the word 'you' and tend to point the finger at the other person. They close down the lines of communication. Jakob says to Sara, "Your problem is that **you** are always telling me what I'm doing wrong."	To eliminate misunderstandings, Top 20s clarify what the other has said by paraphrasing. They describe the problem by using 'I' statements which take the focus off what the other person has done to us and reduces our tendency to blame. 'I' statements cause a less defensive response and keep the communication channels open.

'I' statements follow the pattern: I feel _____ when _____.

"You" Statements	"I" Statements
"You always leave your toys on the floor. "	"I feel angry when I'm the one cleaning up your toys."
"You never put the milk away."	"I get upset when the milk stays out on the table and spoils."
"You're always so loud and noisy."	"I get a headache when the noise is so loud."

What do we GET?

Toe-Toe	Heart-Heart
The result when someone loses in a conflict is resentment and loss of trust. When this happens, the conflict is likely to become worse. Unresolved, it is buried alive and usually resurfaces in revenge. Both parties experience Lose-Lose.	When two people sincerely seek what is beneficial for each other, their relationship improves because trust and respect have grown. By working together they will frequently find a new solution that is better than what each person originally had.

The result for Jakob and Sara is an ongoing stress on their relationship and fearful children who are emotionally hurt and powerless.

Toe-to-toe resulted in Jakob, Sara and their family experiencing conflict but not resolution. Had they been able to practice Heart-to-heart, the experience would have been in some way beneficial to all family members and provided them with hope for resolving future conflicts.

NINE INEFFECTIVE ROLES

Over years of repeating behaviors during conflict situations, we often develop specific roles. Although frequently used by parents, the following nine roles are highly ineffective when carried out in family conflicts. No resolution comes from these behaviors. They are hurtful, keep relationships in constant battle and increase the intensity of a problem.

The Historian: Never lets the child forget past mistakes and reminds her on a regular basis as new mistakes are made: "Every time you try to pour your juice, you always spill."

The Mind Reader: Proposes to know what the child is thinking and answers for the child: "I know you are thinking you can get away with this."

The Shrink: Analyzes behavior in a way that makes a diagnosis about the child instead of the behavior: "You're a selfish brat who will wind up in a psychiatrist's office someday."

The Grammar Teacher: Corrects language or behavior rather than dealing with the real issue: "When will you stop mumbling and talk so I can understand you."

The Judge: Judges behavior as being bad or wrong and gives out the punishment due: "Not sharing is selfish. You will have your toys taken away from you for the rest of the day."

The Apathetic: Gives up and gives in to the undesirable behavior: "Do whatever you want. I don't care, just leave me alone."

The Know-it-All: Knows all the answers and doesn't let the child give reasons for the behavior: "Let me tell you what you need to do. You have to apologize and give up your turn."

The Drill Sergeant: Makes the child stand at attention when being spoken to and gives commands as to behaviors accepted and not accepted: "Don't move when I'm talking to you. Don't you roll your eyes at me."

The Lawyer: Talks over all other arguments: "I don't care what you have to say about it. The evidence says that you made your brother cry."

These roles may help us win battles, but not resolve conflict. In fact, they usually tend to increase the conflict or bury it alive to come back later with greater negative energy. Top 20 Parents know when they are in danger of taking on one of these roles, setting the stage for Toe-to-toe confrontation rather than Heart-to-heart resolutions.

A FAMILY PROBLEM SOLVING STRATEGY

Working together is essential to building an effective family. As we have seen, a Bottom 80 Toe-to-toe approach fractures family unity. A Top 20 Heart-to-heart approach builds unity through cooperation and respect.

The following, from *Before Push Comes to Shove: Building Conflict Resolution Skills with Children*, is an example of a Heart-to-heart strategy that not only helps families resolve conflicts but teaches children of all ages how to find solutions to problems.[11]

1. Bring together all people involved in the conflict. Ask: What is the conflict? Listen for and respect feelings without blaming or judging.
2. Brainstorm solutions. Ask: What solutions could we try?
3. Choose acceptable solutions and create a plan of action. Ask: Who is responsible for what?
4. Set a time to evaluate the plan. Ask: How did our plan work?

Jakob and Sara's Toe-to-toe conflict was flaring out of control because they saw each other as the problem. By using the Heart-to-heart process the family can work together and the outcome of their story might look like this:

After the vase crashes, the family gathers in the living room to discuss the conflict. Two problems are identified: the parents' need to do chores and the children's need to play. Together the family brainstorms many possible solutions:

1. the children help with chores and afterwards the family goes to the park,
2. the parents stagger chores so that the children can be monitored,
3. acceptable indoor game choices are identified.

Solutions are chosen and a new schedule is planned. At an agreed upon future date, the plan is evaluated by the family.

"The aim of an argument or discussion should not be victory, but progress."

–Joseph Joubert

DEVELOPMENTAL NEWS FLASH!

Making the transition from conflict to resolution is difficult for all, especially young children. This shift requires being able to think about more than one thing at a time, being able to plan actions in advance, and having empathy in how others see events and situations. Young children have to experience conflict in order to experiment with the best ways to manage it. Children take what they see and hear about conflict and try out ideas, learning through experience. Therefore, keeping children from all conflict is not in their Best Interest.

• **Young children are egocentric.** A child's inability to look at the perspective of others may look like selfishness. A child cannot easily think how experiences and situations will be seen or felt by another person.

• **Young children are concrete learners.** In dealing with conflict resolution, concepts such as trust, sharing, fairness, respect and forgiveness are abstract and difficult for young children to grasp.

• **Young children have trouble connecting cause and effect.** They may find it difficult to connect behavior and consequence in events and relationships. They may also have trouble predicting how their behaviors might affect a future situation.

• **Empathy in young children is immature.** While empathy is an essential piece to being able to participate in conflict resolution, young children may have difficulty responding to the emotions of others. They will often need to be guided as empathy emerges.

• **The impulse control area of the brain is immature in young children.** They have many emotional impulses and quickly act on them. Throwing toys in anger or hitting others are simply actions without thought. Young children can be guided to see that impulsive actions have consequences and that they can gain control over their impulses.

BUILDING CONFLICT RESOLUTION SKILLS

Many authors and parenting experts have addressed how conflict can be resolved in families. According to Second Step, a violence prevention curriculum, three areas that can be nurtured in children to help them as they encounter conflict are emotional awareness, empathy and impulse control. [12]

Emotional Awareness is developed when emotions are acknowledged and labeled. Although children begin with a very limited vocabulary about emotions, parents can expand that vocabulary and emotional awareness by:

• Making comments such as: "I see you are upset that the toy broke." "It's ok to be sad."

- Looking at photos with your child to discuss emotions and the facial and body cues that communicate the emotions.

- Narrating emotional situations for our children: "Look at your sister's face right now. She has tears on her cheeks and her mouth is turned down. She is sad because you pushed her when you were angry."

As difficult as it might be, we must acknowledge strong emotions in our children and not dismiss or mislabel them. As parents we deny emotions when we scoop up an obviously distraught child and say:

"Stop crying. There's nothing to be upset about."
"Hush, you're ok."

Empathy is built when parents point out the cause and effect of emotional situations. Whenever a parent talks about how others are feeling about events and situations, a child learns to understand the perspective of others. For example: "When you fling the books in anger, your brother can get hurt and cry" or "Cyndi gets scared when you throw toys. She feels like she doesn't want to play at our house."

Impulse Control is another conflict resolution skill that children can learn. A young child will likely lash out with action immediately after feeling a strong emotion. Examples are biting immediately after a toy is grabbed away or hitting someone when frustrated.

Impulse control is learned over time as a child slowly comes to insert 'thought' between 'emotion' and 'action'.

- We can anticipate when the child's 'action' is about to occur and then intervene with narration that acknowledges the emotions involved. "Whoa! I see an angry face and hand. Looks like you are upset that he's playing with your favorite car." Eventually one can almost 'see the wheels turning' as a child looks to check in with the adult before hitting or grabbing because a thought has been inserted before immediate action.

- We can talk with our children about how the brain is involved in body actions. For example, "Tell your brain to stop those legs from kicking." Games where the action stops and starts, like musical chairs, slow-motion walking, or Red Light-Green Light, will give a child practice in body control.

- We can give children appropriate words and actions for conflict situations. Instead of just saying "Use your words," give actual phrases for specific situations: "Can I have a turn next," "I get angry when you take my toy," or "Stop pushing me." We also need to tell our children what to do when words don't work. Appropriate actions when words don't work would be to walk away or get help from an adult. Waiting for a turn, trading toys or substituting a toy or activity are better options than hitting or pushing.

MODELING DIGNITY AND RESPECT

At times we may not get the outcome we originally desired in a conflict situation. However, as Top 20 Parents we can always deal with a conflict in a way that does not damage a relationship and will retain dignity and respect for ourselves and others. By responding this way, we are also modeling for our children how to maintain their dignity and respect in conflict situations.

TIME FOR ACTION!

For Parents to Do:

1. Analyze how you have handled family conflicts in the past. How would you like to handle conflict in the future?

2. How do you respond to conflict with your children when you are in public? Does being in public affect your ability to problem solve?

3. Practice 'I' statements to communicate your feelings about a situation. Analyze how this strategy helps in resolving conflict.

4. Find early childhood books (see Appendix C, p. 124) to reinforce messages about resolving conflict.

To Do with Your Child:

1. Observe how your child reacts in conflict. Do his behaviors resemble your own when faced with conflict?

2. Recognize, label and acknowledge the emotions of your child.

3. Look for opportunities to point out nonverbal cues, such as tears, facial expressions and gestures, that communicate emotions in other people.

4. Role play conflict situations, practicing using appropriate words and appropriate actions when words don't work.

5. Observe your child and try to anticipate when inappropriate actions will occur in order to intervene and stop the behavior.

6. Practice the Heart-to-heart Conflict Resolution Process in your family (p. 104).

107

CHAPTER 17

Getting Back on Course
Making Something Better After Making It Worse

*"Mistakes are a fact of life.
It is the response to error that counts."*
–Nikki Giovanni

A negative Below the Line atmosphere filled the Hernandez household. A half hour ago the siblings were calling each other names, Dad was threatening the kids and yelling at them to stop slamming doors, and Mom had a headache and was in tears.

Later grilling hamburgers for supper in the backyard, Dad knew he had to get the family back on course. Having often used humor in his life to cope with stress, he noticed Halloween costumes hanging in the garage.

When the children went to the patio to complain about how hungry they were, they erupted with laughter. They saw Dad in a clown wig and red nose happily flipping burgers. Mom and the children joined in the fun by finding costumes to wear to dinner. Dad's hamburgers were better than ever.

Every family has emotionally intense events: tantrums, tornadoes, sibling brawls or over-reacting parents. How can a family recover and move on without getting stuck in the negativity?

Like Mr. Hernandez, Top 20s desire and know how to make something better after they have made it worse. Rather than staying stuck in yuck, Top 20 Parents use three simple strategies to get beyond negative family experiences and feelings to reconciliation and a more satisfactory life.

START OVERS

Have you ever said something and wished you could 'catch' the words before they entered someone's ears? Unfortunately we're not quick enough to do that, but we can be wise enough to make it better by starting over.

When filming movies, actors repeat scenes again and again to create better versions of a scene. When the director says, "Cut", everyone knows it's time to Start Over. In families, Start Overs can look much the same.

Take 1

Fran came down the steps carrying the basket of dirty laundry. For the second time this week she stumbled at the bottom step over the roller blades left by her daughter. Angrily, Fran found her daughter. "Karley, I'm forever falling over your roller blades. I nearly broke my neck. Get rid of them now and go to your room."

"No. I won't!" said Karley stomping her feet.

"That's it. No more play time for you tonight. I've had enough of your lip. Go to your room and stay there."

After Karley ran to her room, Fran began to think about what went wrong. She remembered telling her daughter to bring the roller blades in from outside but hadn't designated an inside storage spot. Realizing Karley wouldn't recognize the danger of leaving roller blades on the steps, Fran went to her daughter's room.

Take 2

"Karley, can we do a Start Over?"

"OK," said Karley, still angry but willing to improve the situation.

Karley went back to where she had been playing as Fran set the roller blades at the bottom of the steps.

Calling her daughter to the steps, she said, "Karley, I was carrying the laundry down the steps and almost stepped on the roller blades. What do you think would have happened next?"

"You'd fall and could get hurt," said Karley.

"Where can you put the roller blades so they're not dangerous?"

"Umm, I could put them in the closet," said Karley, warming to the idea of being asked to problem solve. "Or you could give me a sports bag like Daddy uses for his basketball stuff."

"That's a good idea. For now, please put them in the closet."

By using a Start Over, Fran and Karley made something better after they had made something worse. They felt better and changed the tone of the rest of the evening. Furthermore, Karley learned what she can do in the future with her roller blades.

Start Overs express hope in the relationship by showing care and concern about the feelings of others when interactions go poorly.

A parent can introduce the Start Over in different ways:

"This hasn't gone the way I'd like it to. Can we start over?"

"I don't feel good about this. I think we can make this better. Let's try it again."

FORGIVING AND FORGETTING

Stephen Covey believes that the ultimate test of a relationship comes in forgiving. We will always be a victim until we forgive. When we truly forgive, we open the channels through which trust and unconditional love can flow. Forgiveness is a deposit in the Trust Fund.

"Don't let the sun go down while you are still angry."

–Ephesians 4:26

When an event is over and forgiven, it needs to be laid to rest or forgotten. To bring the matter up again would be to negate the progress a family has made in reconciling. The Hernandez family was able to move on because the original fight was forgiven and forgotten. The outcome would have been much different if during dinner Dad rehashed the fight again to lay blame.

GENTLE HUMOR

Humor can bring about reconciliation in a family. Positive humor defuses stressful situations and mends hurt feelings and misunderstandings. Healthy families can laugh with one another, using a funny situation as a shared experience. The Hernandez family's costumed dinner is a great example of sharing laughter.

"Talk happiness. The world is sad enough."

–Ella Wheeler Wilcox

Bottom 80 families laugh at one another. Their personal shortcomings become family jokes. Many Hits are given in the disguise of humor. If we are committed to making things better after making things worse, we need to watch the tone of our humor. **Top 20 families laugh at the situation,** but not at the people involved.

While making Thanksgiving dinner, Shari left the boiled potatoes soaking in the water. Mashing them later, she realized they had soaked too long and turned into mush. During dinner, people said, "Pass the mush," with a good-natured twinkle in their eyes. The grandmothers used the experience to talk about their own cooking disasters. A new family bonding tradition emerged with cooking disasters being told every year.

DEVELOPMENTAL NEWS FLASH!!!

• **Young children are concrete learners.** Children will have trouble talking about the abstract concept of forgiveness. Start Overs physically reenact a situation concretely so that children can learn about cause and effect and relationships in a 'hands on' way.

• **Young children have trouble connecting their actions with the results they get.** Children don't always know what details to focus on the first time an event plays out. Start Overs help a child focus on what was missed the first time, builds empathy and gives parents the opportunity to discuss how an event looks from another's point of view.

Our parenting journey is long and arduous. Because we sometimes act on limited information, we will make mistakes along the way. In and of themselves, these detours are not failures. How we respond to these episodes, however, will determine whether or not a small wrong turn takes a family completely off course.

For Parents to Do:

1. Remember a time when you regretted saying something to another person. If you could start over again, how would you change what you said?

2. How has forgiveness brought you peace in the past? Do you forget past wrongs or keep bringing an offense up with a family member?

3. When was the last time you were silly or had a good laugh? What keeps you from being silly or using humor to diffuse situations?

To Do with Your Child:

1. Practice Start Overs with your child. Then when a real situation occurs, she will be familiar with the process.

2. Cultivate times for silliness, fun and humor with your child. Try to share a laugh every day.

3. Look for opportunities to say "I forgive you" or "I'm sorry" after an event has taken the family off course.

4. Hug your child often.

CHAPTER 18

~~The End~~/The Beginning

Remember back to the birth of your child. How profound and life changing that was! But little did any of us who have become parents realize on that day all the joy and anxiety, memorable moments and challenges, gratitude and disappointments we would experience during our parenting journey.

If your child could have talked on the day of his birth, he might have said something like, "I'm here. Now what?" What those four little words mean is: "I've gotten this far but now I need a lot of help."

What our children are asking for is what this book is really all about—leadership. Parenting is a specific form of leadership that takes children on a journey of self-discovery. Their discovery of their own true identity requires that we believe in them, value them for who they are and help them develop their own unique potential.

In order to do this, we must be able to trust ourselves. "When we trust ourselves," writes M. J. Ryan, "we know that we are good enough as we are—with our gifts and strengths, with our foibles and failings. We are not fearful of making a mistake because we know we will survive, maybe even grow from the experience. We believe that what we have to offer—our essence—is what is being called for…all that is being asked of each of us is to be as real as we can be."[13]

To the extent that we are 'as real as we can be', we become happy, responsible and emotionally healthy people. As such, we are able to lead our children to discover their own power to be happy, responsible and emotionally healthy.

"With self-trust," says Ryan, "we understand that power and peace is (sic) found in 'response-ability', our capacity to meet life as it comes at us. When we believe in our ability to respond, we don't fight against the wildness of life because we know we'll handle what comes our way when it arrives." [14]

We hope that what you have experienced in *Top 20 Parents* will help you take a giant step in your parenting journey "to meet life" and help your child do the same.

Star Qualities Activities
Bringing the Stars Down to Earth: A How-to Guide

Knowing what the Star Qualities are and their definitions is a good start in becoming a Top 20 Parent. But how do we polish these skills to make them shine for our children? How do we bring the stars down to earth? Here are fifteen Star Qualities and activities for developing these qualities.

"The highest reward for a person's toil is not what they get for it, but what they become by it."

John Ruskin

Courageous: to respond with meaningful action in spite of fear.

As parents we must be courageous to overcome the fear of failing to be good parents, being unpopular with our child or being judged by others. Fear can lead us to shut down or respond in inappropriate ways. As we grow in courage, we will be role models for our children to do likewise.

1. List the things you fear, such as heights or bugs. How can you let your child feel courageous about these things nonetheless?

2. What parenting issue frightens or challenges you? Picture this issue playing out over time in two ways: **with** courageous action to resolve it and **without** courageous action. Which scenario do you prefer? What support do you need to be courageous?

3. Introduce emotions like fear, dislike, bravery and courage by labeling them when seen in books, movies or real life. Acknowledge your child's emotions and don't belittle her real fears. Point out how courageous actions can lead to positive results.

4. Share with your child a time that you did something courageous though fearful, like public speaking or confessing to breaking a window as a child. Watch for and praise examples of courage in your child.

Creative: inventive, full of ideas; using ideas to solve problems.

1. Creativity takes many forms: cooking, decorating, keeping a budget, household repairs, keeping peace within the family. Think of ways you are creative.

2. Analyze your conversations with your child. Are you providing a safe environment for him to share creative ideas? Strive to ask more questions about his opinions, ideas and interests.

3. Look for opportunities to let your child make choices: choosing clothes, picking a book to read, selecting paint colors.

4. Self expression is part of the creative process. Encourage your child to be self-expressive in different ways with crayons, paint, play dough, blocks, glue work and music shakers.

5. Practice this problem solving process with your child. Situations like not having someone to play with, not having a favorite ice cream flavor, or a broken toy are opportunities to practice this process.
   A. What is the problem?
   B. What solutions can we try?
   C. What are the good and bad points of these solutions?
   D. What do you think of the solution that we tried?

6. Brainstorm lists such as all the vehicles that use wheels or all the animals your child knows. Playing with these lists develops creativity.

Curious: having a desire to know and learn; willing to leave what is comfortable to explore the unknown.

Young children are naturally curious. They learn best through exploration and hands on experience. As young children develop, curiosity is the motivation that keeps children learning and maturing.

1. When was the last time you experimented with a new food, explored a new place, or tried a new hobby or something else new? Encourage your own curiosity. What would you like to know more about?

2. Play with puzzles or games that require exploring options to find solution. Don't solve these for your child. Use questions to lead her to find the answers.

3. Use encouraging language when it comes to exploration and discovery. For example, "Hey, that's interesting. Let's find out more about it."

4. Take time to answer your child's many questions about everything. Answers can be brief in keeping with development.

Emotional Awareness: recognizing and dealing with one's own emotions and the emotions of others; being in touch with feelings and thoughts.

1. Think back to how emotions were handled in your family of origin. How does that affect how you deal with emotions now? Is there anything you want to change when you interact with your child regarding emotions?

2. Talk to your child about your emotions. Openly express how events and behaviors affect you. Label your child's emotions as they occur.

3. Play 'Same and Different' with your child. First play with objects, looking for attributes like hard, soft, shiny, bumpy, big and little. Then play 'Same and Different' while looking at the emotions on people's faces in photos and illustrations.

4. Label and discuss feelings as they occur in books and movies. To promote empathy, ask your child what he would feel in similar situations.

Focused: to stay fixed on a goal or task; filtering out constant stimuli and paying attention to what's important.

Temperament can play a role in the ability to focus, making it easier for some than others. Development needs to guide our expectations for the focus abilities of young children. It is very difficult for young children to focus on anything for very long.

1. How hard is it for you to focus? What distracts you? What role does your temperament play in focusing?

2. Note how long your child can focus on an activity. Keeping development in mind, playfully encourage her to extend an experience for a few minutes more.

3. Young children have a hard time focusing on more than one direction at a time. Give your child funny, playful directions to encourage focus: wiggle your nose. Increase the amount of directions and their complexity over time.

4. Give your child something to look for in a book, movie or place before the activity begins. For example, "When we get to the museum, look for the statue of the monkey and tell me when you see it."

Optimistic: being hopeful; seeing the positive in people, situations and events; belief in the capacity to bring about positive outcomes.

Temperament plays a role in optimism. The opposite of optimism is negativity, highlighted by blame, anger, a lack of responsibility and victimization. One can learn to think optimistically.

1. How optimistic are you in daily life? What are your negative habits that keep you from being optimistic? When you find yourself Below the Line, what Trampolines can you use to get back Above the Line and into a state of optimism?

2. Share with your child times when apparent disasters and failures turned out positive for you or your child in the long run.

3. Share a hopeful vision of your child's future with him that includes education, friends and family support. Looking at birth pictures is often a good conversation starter for this activity.

4. Talk to your child about what might be scary or exciting in life. Plan on ways to look forward to the future like marking a calendar or hanging a motivating photo on the refrigerator. Optimism grows when one can look forward to or hope for something.

Organized: able to keep life in order so problems and conflicts are limited.

1. Analyze how your home life is organized. Are there areas that need to be worked on, such as budget, chores, shopping lists or mail clutter?

2. Analyze why areas of your family's life might be disorganized. For instance, overtired parents may have a hard time keeping the house clean. Problem solve ways to be more organized in your life.

3. Guide your child to put things back where they belong after each use. Role model by putting things away after use.

4. Introduce your child to the concept of time by discussing the length of activities. Discuss schedules and calendars. For example, "Today we will go to the store and then after lunch we can go to the playground."

5. Enlist your child in organizing family activities. Ask them to help with grocery lists, clipping useful coupons or reorganizing cupboards.

Outgoing: friendly and sociable; able to relate to the emotions and behaviors of others.

1. Are you outgoing or do you have to work at it? Think about what brought you to your present skill level.

2. Increase interactions of family members during meals, chores and TV time.

3. Ask your child's opinions frequently about choices, feelings, favorites, and guesses. Build conversation skills by encouraging her to take polls of family members about favorite foods, colors or sports teams.

4. Teach your child manners and social behaviors that can be practiced on the phone, at stores or in conversations. For example, saying thank you to the cashier at the store or "How are you feeling today, Grandma?"

Persistent: to persevere with effort until completion; follow through and finish.

It may seem like some people have overnight success. However, tremendous effort and persistence usually goes into achieving what often looks easy to an outsider. Perseverance is the key difference between those who try and those who succeed.

1. Think about how you or your child feel after accomplishing a task.

2. Point out to your child examples of persistence, hard work and endurance when you see it in people like carpenters working, athletes training or musicians practicing.

3. Share with your child times when you stuck to a project even when you were frustrated, like house or car maintenance. Tell of a time when you had to try over and over again.

4. Label feelings, such as frustrated, excited, confident and proud, as you narrate your child's persistence in tasks and activities.

"Never do anything for a child that a child can do for himself or herself."

Magda Gerber

5. Allow your child to finish tasks, even when frustration and fatigue occur. Resist the urge to finish these projects for him.

Proactive: taking actions to deal with situations before they become a problem; analyzing **why** things happened last time and predicting **how** to change outcomes for the better.

In parenting, being proactive means analyzing and anticipating problems and then preparing for events and situations. For example, running errands during a child's nap time without anticipating problem behavior will lead to a frustrated parent and an exhausted, uncooperative child. Next time, a proactive parent might run errands before or after naptime, giving both parent and child a better experience.

1. Analyze trouble spots in your family. Be proactive to prevent problems next time. For example, if there is friction in the morning, set out clothes the night before and have backpacks ready at the door.

2. Narrate 'cause and effect' in problem situations. For example, "When you take your brother's toy, it makes him feel angry. Then your brother hits you and you feel sad." Lead your child to predict and change outcomes: "Next time, ask your brother if you can have a turn with his toy. You'll both feel happy if you can take turns."

Responsible: to do what is right and follow through; to be accountable, reliable and dependable.

1. Share with your child an example when you were responsible. Your example as a responsible adult is a powerful learning tool.

2. Give your child chores in keeping with age appropriate ability like sorting and matching socks, stuffing clothes in the laundry machines, stirring cake mix, and setting the table. Help him to follow through and complete the task at hand. Resist the urge to take over the responsibility and finish the task for him.

3. Create a chart of your child's morning and evening routines, such as brushing teeth and making the bed, so that self-care responsibilities can be seen at a glance to encourage follow through.

Self-Confident: belief in oneself, belief that "I can."

1. Trace your child's body on a large piece of paper. Create a photo book or a ME poster about your child. Display these representations of her in a place of honor.

2. Post your child's artwork. Take pictures of his block towers, play dough sculptures, preschool performances or other accomplishments to indicate your value of his efforts.

3. Be specific with praise: "Thank you for putting away the blocks so quickly when I asked." Let your child hear you talk to others about her strengths.

4. Knowing that completing a task on one's own builds confidence, give your child many opportunities to do things for himself.

Self-Disciplined: in control of emotions and actions; delaying gratification to wait for an anticipated outcome.

"I am indeed a king, because I know how to rule myself."
Pietro Aretino

Our expectations of a child's self-control should be developmentally appropriate. In young children the impulse control part of their brain is still developing, affecting their actions and behaviors. Learning how to get one's brain to tell the body to stop doing certain actions will take many years but the process should begin at a young age.

1. Self-discipline is difficult. How well can you control or postpone your own desires in order to accomplish parenting goals, like giving up some TV viewing to get your child to bed at a decent time or working extra shifts to pay for an upcoming family trip?

2. Make a game of practicing self-discipline and impulse control with your child. Set up situations where she can complete tasks before having a desirable object or event. For example, "Can you go five minutes without poking your brother before we go to play in the park?" or "Can we get through the store without you asking for gum before having lunch at the restaurant?" Increase self-discipline by asking her to complete tasks without a reward.

3. Encourage self-discipline by asking your child to have a plan for the day and review it as the day progresses. For example, "You said you wanted to draw with crayons before lunch. Did you do that?"

4. Putting things away consistently after using them requires self-discipline. Require your child to clean up after activities, giving age appropriate help as needed. Provide the means of storage (bins, shelves or hooks) for him to be able to put toys and belongings away.

Self-Motivated: being a 'self-starter'; seeing what needs to be done without waiting for others to lead; interested in doing what needs to happen.

Bottom 80 thinkers believe motivation comes before action. They only act when they're motivated. When Top 20 thinkers aren't motivated, they don't wait around. Knowing that when they act motivation sometimes kicks in, they start the project and motivation usually follows.

1. Think about ways for your home to be a place for your child to explore and start activities independently. For example, create an area for messy art projects with access to supplies or create a cozy reading area with inviting picture books that your child can pick by herself.

2. Encourage an excitement for learning and exploration by finding ways for your child to try one new thing each day: a new food, new music, a different drive home or looking out a different window to look for birds. Praise him when he explores something new on his own.

3. Go for Discovery Walks inside stores, public buildings or near construction sites. Use a magnifying glass to see more. Tape record sounds to enjoy later. Collect artifacts like sand and leaves for a later piece of collage artwork.

Spiritual: to be connected with one's true self, values and principles by which to live; searching for something beyond ourselves that gives meaning to life. A strong spirituality will keep us from being influenced by false messages.

1. Include your child in discussions about your spiritual beliefs from an early age. Recognize and point out the spiritual beliefs of others, often exhibited through their actions.

2. Because of their curiosity, young children ask questions of a spiritual nature, like "Who made the clouds?" or "Why do people die?" Think about how you might answer these questions. Keep meals TV-free so that you can talk while you eat.

3. Make an effort to align your child's experiences to your beliefs and make sure he sees the connection. For instance, read to him every day if you value reading or give to charities if you believe in giving to others.

Temperament Rating Scale

Circle the number on the top scale that best identifies where you are for each trait.[15] Circle the number on the bottom scale that best identifies where your child is for each trait.

Activity: the daily proportion of active periods (moving, running, fidgeting) and quiet periods (resting, relaxing, playing quietly). An active child may be noisy and constantly engaged in action.

> **Parent:** Low Activity 1 2 3 4 5 High Activity
> **Child:** Low Activity 1 2 3 4 5 High Activity

Regularity: the predictability or unpredictability of biological functions (hunger, sleeping and bowel elimination) affecting a person's ability to cope with schedules and routines. An irregular child may be difficult for a parent seeking to establish a family routine.

> **Parent:** Regularity 1 2 3 4 5 Irregularity
> **Child:** Regularity 1 2 3 4 5 Irregularity

Approach vs Withdrawal: the first reaction to a new situation, person or thing. Approachability is seen in a child whose first reactions may include smiling, engagement and interest in a new experience. Withdrawal reactions are crying, moving away, refusal to try, tantrums or stomach aches.

> **Parent:** Approaches 1 2 3 4 5 Withdraws
> **Child:** Approaches 1 2 3 4 5 Withdraws

Adaptability: the ease to which a person is able to adapt to change in schedules, routines or situations. A child with low adaptability expresses long-term levels of stress, disappointment, confusion, uncooperativeness or anger.

> **Parent:** Low Adaptability 1 2 3 4 5 High Adaptability
> **Child:** Low Adaptability 1 2 3 4 5 High Adaptability

Sensory Threshold: the intensity of reaction to how things taste, feel, smell, look and sound. A sensitive child reacts to bright lights, loud music, the emotions of others, temperature, colors, tags in clothing and food textures leading quickly to over stimulation.

> **Parent:** Low Threshold 1 2 3 4 5 High Threshold
> **Child:** Low Threshold 1 2 3 4 5 High Threshold

Quality of Mood: the balance of time spent happy, smiling, optimistic, content and social compared to the time spent serious, analytical, withdrawn, sad or cranky. A child with a predominantly negative mood may be whiny, critical, tearful and seem ungrateful.

> **Parent:** Positive Mood 1 2 3 4 5 Negative Mood
> **Child:** Positive Mood 1 2 3 4 5 Negative Mood

Intensity of Reactions: the strength of a positive or negative emotional reaction to events, people or things. An intense child's powerful reactions are characterized by loud laughter and happy outbursts or screams, tears and tantrums. Low intensity is characterized by calm, quiet and mild reactions.

> **Parent:** Low Intensity 1 2 3 4 5 High Intensity
> **Child:** Low Intensity 1 2 3 4 5 High Intensity

Distractibility: the degree to which a person is distracted by people, colors, noises and objects in the environment. Because a highly distractible child cannot filter outside stimuli, he loses focus on tasks or parental requests.

> **Parent:** Low Distractibility 1 2 3 4 5 High Distractibility
> **Child:** Low Distractibility 1 2 3 4 5 High Distractibility

Persistence: the continuation of an activity in the face of obstacles and difficulties. A persistent child is focused on completing an activity without quitting. She can stay determined for a long time, regardless of a lack of success or rewards.

> **Parent:** Low Persistence 1 2 3 4 5 High Persistence
> **Child:** Low Persistence 1 2 3 4 5 High Persistence

Children's Literature Book List

STORIES ABOUT MESSAGES

The Little Engine that Could, Watty Piper (1930) New York: Platt and Munk Publishers

The Ugly Duckling, Hans Christian Anderson and Jerry Pinkney (1999) New York: Morrow Junior Books

Chicken Little, public domain (1998) New York: Harper Festival

The Emperor's New Clothes, Hans Christian Anderson (1949) New York: Houghton Mifflin

BOOKS ABOUT MISTAKES

I Love You Forever, Robert Munsch (1986) Willowdale, Ontario: Firefly Books Ltd.

Mama, Do You Love Me?, Barbara M. Joosse (1991) San Francisco: Chronicle Books

Papa, Do You Love Me?, Barbara M. Joosse (2005) San Francisco: Chronicle Books

Runaway Bunny, Margaret Wise Brown (1942) New York: Harper and Row, Publishers, Inc.

Peter Rabbit Tales, Beatrix Potter (1996) London: Frederick Warne and Co.

The Best Mistake Ever! and Other Stories, Richard Scarry (1984) New York: Random House

Foolish Rabbit's Big Mistake, Rafe Martin (1985) New York: Putnam and Grosset Group

Nobody's Perfect: A book About Making Mistakes (1993) Norwich, England: Grolier Books

BOOKS ABOUT CONFLICT RESOLUTION

Words are not for Hurting, Elizabeth Verdick (2004) Minneapolis: Free Spirit Publishing

Feet are not for Kicking, Elizabeth Verdick (2004) Minneapolis: Free Spirit Publishing

Hands are not for Hitting, Martine Agassi (2002) Minneapolis: Free Spirit Publishing

Teeth are not for Biting, Elizabeth Verdick (2003) Minneapolis: Free Spirit Publishing

I can Share, Karen Katz (2004) New York: Grosset and Dunlap

No Hitting!, Karen Katz (2004) New York: Grosset and Dunlap

A Bargain for Frances, Russell Hoban (1970) New York: Harper Collins

Where the Wild Things Are, Maurice Sendak (1963) New York: Harper Collins

The Sneeches and Other Stories, Dr. Suess (1961) New York: Random House

Berenstain Bears and the Trouble with Friends, Stan Berenstain and Jan Berenstain (1986) New York: Random House

How to Take the Grrrr Out of Anger, Elizabeth Verdick and Marjorie Lisovskis (2003) Minneapolis: Free Spirit Publishing

Dude, That's Rude!: (Get Some Manners), Pamela Espeland, Elizabeth Verdick and Steve Mark (2007) Minneapolis: Free Spirit Publishing

BOOKS ABOUT FEELINGS

Quick as a Cricket, Audrey Wood (1982) Swindon, England: Child's Play

The Way I Feel, Janan Cain (2000) Seattle: Parenting Press, Inc.

If You're Angry and Your Know It, Cecily Kaiser (2004) New York: Scholastic

Sometimes I Feel Like a Mouse: A Book about Feelings, Jeanne Modesitt(1996) New York: Scholastic

Footnotes

1. Adele Faber and Elaine Mazlish. *How to Talk So Kids Will Listen and Listen So Kids Will Talk.* New York: Harper Collins Publisher, 1980, p. 1.

2. Daniel Goleman. *Emotional Intelligence: Why It Can Matter More Than IQ.* New York: Bantam Books, 1995, p. 33-42.

3. Ibid. p. 43-44.

4. John Gottman and Joan DeClaire. *Raising An Emotionally Intelligent Child: The Heart of Parenting.* New York: Simon & Schuster, 1997, p. 63.

5. Thomas Lickona. *Raising Good Children.* New York: Bantam Books, 1983, p. 11-13.

6. Robert J. Sternberg. *Successful Intelligence.* New York: Penguin Group, 1996, p. 12.

7. Lucille Gutshewsky Bauer, Elizabeth A. Hoodecheck and Diane Schulz Simpson. *Parents Are Teachers: Educator's Manual.* St. Cloud, MN: District 742 Community Education's Early Childhood Family Education Project, revised 1993.

8. Stella Chess and Alexander Thomas. *Know Your Child.* New York: Basic Books, 1987, p. 28-31.

9. Ibid. p. 32-34.

10. Stephen R. Covey. *The 7 Habits of Highly Effective People.* New York: Simon & Schuster, 1990, p. 188.

11. Nancy Carlsson-Paige and Diane E. Levin. *Before Push Comes to Shove: Building Conflict Resolution Skills with Children.* St. Paul, MN: Redleaf Press, 1998, p. 72.

12. *Second Step ®: A Violence Prevention Curriculum Preschool/Kindergarten.* Seattle, WA: Committee For Children, 2002, p. 7-17.

13. M. J. Ryan. *Trusting Yourself.* New York: Broadway Books, 2004, p. 35.

14. Ibid. p. 38.

15. Chess and Thomas, p. 28-31.

Bibliography

Bauer, L. G., Hoodecheck, E. A., Simpson, D. S., Running, C. (revised 1993). *Parents Are Teachers: Educator's Manual*, St. Cloud, MN: District 742 Community Education's Early Childhood Family Education Project. For further information, contact Ellen Kearns, 320-253-5828.

Benson, P. L., Galbraith, J., and Espeland, P. (1998). *What Teens Need to Succeed,* Minneapolis: Free Spirit Publishing, Inc.

Bernabei, P., Cody, T., Cole, M., Cole, M. and Sweeney,W. (2004). *Top 20 Teens: Discovering the Best-Kept Thinking, Learning and Communicating Secrets of Successful Teenagers,* St. Paul: Top 20 Training.

Bloom, B.S. (Ed.) (1956). *Taxonomy of educational objectives: The classification of educational goals: Handbook 1, cognitive domain.* New York: Longmans, Green.

Bredekamp, S. and Copple, C. (Eds.) (1997). *Developmentally Appropriate Practice.* Washington, DC: National Association for the Education of Young Children.

Carey, W. B. (1997). *Understanding Your Child's Temperament.* New York: MacMillan.

Carlsson-Paige, N. and Levin, D. E. (1998). *Before Push Comes to Shove: Building Conflict Resolution Skills with Children.* St. Paul: Redleaf Press.

Chapman, G. D. and Campbell, R. (1992). *The Five Love Languages of Children.* Chicago: Northfield Publishing.

Chess, S. and Thomas, A. (1986). *Temperament in Clinical Practice.* New York: Guilford.

Covey, S. (1990). *The 7 Habits of Highly Effective People.* New York: Simon & Schuster.

Crain, W. (1980). *Theories of Development.* Englewood Cliffs, New Jersey: Prentice Hall.

Curran, D. (1983). *Traits of a Healthy Family.* Minneapolis: Winston Press, Inc.

Curran, D. (1985). *Stress and the Healthy Family,* Minneapolis: Winston Press, Inc.

Faber, A. and Mazlish, E. (1980). *How to Talk so Kids will Listen and Listen so Kids will Talk*. New York: Avon Books.

Gardner, H. (1983). *Frames of Mind: The Theory of Multiple Intelligences*. New York: BasicBooks.

Goleman, D. (1995). *Emotional Intelligence: Why It Can Matter More than IQ*. New York: Bantam.

Gottman, J. and DeClaire, J. (1997). *Raising an Emotionally Intelligent Child: The Heart of Parenting*, New York: Simon & Schuster.

Greenspan, S. and Salmon, J. (1995). *The Challenging Child: Understanding, Raising, and Enjoying the Five "Difficult" Types of Children*. New York: Perseus Books.

Kohn, A. (2005). *Unconditional Parenting: Moving from Rewards and Punishments to Love and Reason*. New York: Atria Books.

Lerner, R. M. and Benson, P. L. (Eds.) (2003). *Developmental Assets and Asset-Building Communities: Implications for Research, Policy and Practice*. New York: Plenum Publishers.

Lickona, T. (1983). *Raising Good Children*. New York: Bantam Books.

Mackenzie, R. (2001). *Setting Limits with Your Strong Willed Child: Eliminating Conflict by Establishing Clear, Firm, and Respectful Boundaries*. Roseville, California: Prima Publishing.

Mooney, C. G. (2005). *Use Your Words: How Teacher Talk Helps Children Learn*. St. Paul: Redleaf Press.

Nelson, J., Erwin, C. and Duffy, R. (1998). *Positive Discipline: The First Three Years*. Roseville, CA: Prima Publishing.

Neville, H., Clark, D. and Garob, D. (1997). *Temperament Tools: Working with Your Child's Inborn Traits*. Seattle: Parenting Press, Inc.

Rich, D. (1998). *MegaSkills*. New York: Houghton Mifflin Company.

Roberts, G. (2007). *Early Childhood Indicators of Progress: Minnesota's Early Learning Guidelines for Birth to 3*. St. Paul: Minnesota Department of Human Services and Minnesota Department of Health.

Roberts, G. (2005). *Early Childhood Indicators of Progress: Minnesota's Early Learning Standards*. Roseville, MN: Minnesota Department of Education and Minnesota Department of Human Services.

Scales, P. C., Benson, P. L., Mannes, M. and Nitz, N. R. (2003). *Other People's Kids: Social Expectations and American Adults' Involvement with Children and Adolescents*. New York: Kluwer Academic/Plenum Publishers.

Second Step: A Violence Prevention Curriculum Preschool/Kindergarten (2002). Seattle: Committee for Children.

Seligman, M. E. P., Reivich, K., Jaycox, L., and Gillham, J. (2007). *The Optimistic Child: A Proven Program to safeguard Children Against Depression and Build Lifelong Resilience.* New York: Houghton Mifflin.

Sternberg, R. J. (1996). *Successful Intelligence*. New York: Penguin Group.

Turecki, S. and Tonner, L. (1984). *The Difficult Child: A New Step-By-Step Approach*. New York: Bantam Books.

TOP 20 TRAINING

Provides training and materials to empower youth and adults

- to develop their potential
- to make a positive difference in their lives, relationships and experiences
- to make a positive difference in the lives of others

Top 20 training sessions: Top 20 training sessions are conducted for youth, educators, parents, coaches, social workers and other adults working in a wide variety of businesses, churches and organizations. For a schedule of Top 20 training sessions, go to www.top20training.com. To schedule a training session for your school or organization, contact Top 20 Training at info@top20training.com.

Top 20 books: *Top 20 Teens: Discovering the Best-kept Thinking, Learning & Communicating Secrets of Successful Teenagers*

Top 20 Parents: Raising Happy, Responsible and Emotionally Healthy Children

Top 20 teachers' manuals: Teacher manuals include Top 20 classroom processes, detailed lesson plans for all concepts in the Top 20 Teens book and a handout for students.

Top 20 TLC Teacher Manual: for grades 3-6
Top 20 Teens Teacher Manual: for grades 7-12

If you have questions about Top 20 Training or would like to order books or materials, contact Top 20 Training.

www.top20training.com   info@top20training.com   651-690-5758

BUY A SHARE OF THE FUTURE IN YOUR COMMUNITY

These certificates make great holiday, graduation and birthday gifts that can be personalized with the recipient's name. The cost of one S.H.A.R.E. or one square foot is $54.17. The personalized certificate is suitable for framing and will state the number of shares purchased and the amount of each share, as well as the recipient's name. The home that you participate in "building" will last for many years and will continue to grow in value.

Here is a sample SHARE certificate:

YES, I WOULD LIKE TO HELP!

I support the work that Habitat for Humanity does and I want to be part of the excitement! As a donor, I will receive periodic updates on your construction activities but, more importantly, I know my gift will help a family in our community realize the dream of homeownership. **I would like to SHARE in your efforts against substandard housing in my community!** *(Please print below)*

PLEASE SEND ME _____ SHARES at $54.17 EACH = $ $_____

In Honor Of: _____

Occasion: (Circle One) HOLIDAY BIRTHDAY ANNIVERSARY

OTHER: _____

Address of Recipient: _____

Gift From: _____ *Donor Address:* _____

Donor Email: _____

I AM ENCLOSING A CHECK FOR $ $_____ PAYABLE TO HABITAT FOR HUMANITY OR PLEASE CHARGE MY VISA OR MASTERCARD *(CIRCLE ONE)*

Card Number _____ Expiration Date: _____

Name as it appears on Credit Card _____ Charge Amount $ _____

Signature _____

Billing Address _____

Telephone # Day _____ Eve _____

PLEASE NOTE: Your contribution is tax-deductible to the fullest extent allowed by law.
Habitat for Humanity • P.O. Box 1443 • Newport News, VA 23601 • 757-596-5553
www.HelpHabitatforHumanity.org